_Katharine Whitehorn_

✳✳✳✳✳✳✳✳✳✳✳✳✳✳✳✳✳✳✳✳✳

# COOKING
## _in a Bedsitter_

PENGUIN BOOKS

Penguin Books Ltd, Harmondsworth, Middlesex, England
Penguin Books, 625 Madison Avenue, New York, New York 10022, U.S.A.
Penguin Books Australia Ltd, Ringwood, Victoria, Australia
Penguin Books Canada Ltd, 2801 John Street, Markham, Ontario, Canada L3R 1B4
Penguin Books (N.Z.) Ltd, 182–190 Wairau Road, Auckland 10, New Zealand

—

First published as *Kitchen in the Corner* by MacGibbon & Kee 1961
Published in Penguin Handbooks 1963
Reprinted 1965, 1967, 1968, 1970, 1971, 1972, 1973
Reprinted with revisions 1974
Reprinted 1975, 1976, 1977, 1978, 1979, 1981

—

—

Set, printed and bound in Great Britain
by Cox & Wyman Ltd, Reading
Set in Monotype Imprint

# COOKING IN A BEDSITTER

Katharine Whitehorn is now a columnist of the *Observer*, married and possessed of a perfectly respectable kitchen stove. Before that, however, she cooked on a variety of gas rings, primuses, and hotplates, while working as a publisher's reader, teacher, waitress, cook in a bowling-alley coffee shop, and journalist. She has lived in Finland and America and knows France well; she has written for periodicals as diverse as *Home Notes* and *Picture Post*, *Woman's Own* and the *Spectator* and her collected *Observer* articles are published under the titles *Only on Sundays* and *Sunday Best*. Her other books include *Whitehorn's Social Survival* (1968), *How to Survive in Hospital* (1972), *How to Survive Children* (1975) and *How to Survive in the Kitchen* (1979). She is married to thriller-writer Gavin Lyall, with whom she lives in Hampstead, surrounded by guns, books and (too many) cats; they have two sons.

*please return*

*alex Smith*
*72 Kinmount ave*

*To Pat, Joan,*
*Maija, Josie, and Lali,*
*who taught me to cook —*
*poor things.*

# Contents

# CONTENTS

# ACKNOWLEDGEMENTS

FEW of these recipes are original, and I am hoping that their authors would be no more affronted to see these adaptations of their ideas than the house of Dior would be to see a Dior copy sold down the Edgware Road. But I am hesitant to thank by name authors who might not approve of a great deal of the contents of this book.

No one who has learned to cook in England since the war can fail to owe an enormous amount to Elizabeth David, whose *French Country Cooking*, *Mediterranean Food*, and *Italian Food* are by now accepted classics. And no one whose progress from rabbit to cook has been helped by Evelyn Board's admirable *The Right Way to his Heart* would pass up a chance to thank her for her splendidly humorous and down-to-earth approach to the whole business.

For permission to reproduce copyright material I am grateful to the author and to the publishers, Victor Gollancz, for the passage from *The Dud Avocado* by Elaine Dundy.

I am very grateful to Ann Lyall, Sybil Flinn, and Jo Whitehorn for recipes; and to my mother for most of the basic information in the book and for responding so promptly to S.O.S. pleas for information. And to Gavin Lyall, who contributed the chapter on drink and rescued me from bedsitters for good.

K.E.W.

PART ONE

# COOKING TO
# STAY ALIVE

✳✳✳✳✳✳✳✳✳✳✳✳✳✳✳✳✳✳✳✳✳✳✳✳✳

CHAPTER I

# The Problem – and Some of the Answers

COOKING a decent meal in a bedsitter is not just a matter of finding something that can be cooked over a single gas ring. It is a problem of finding somewhere to put down the fork while you take the lid off the saucepan, and then finding somewhere else to put the lid. It is finding a place to keep the butter where it will not get mixed up with your razor or your hairpins. It is having your hands covered with flour, and a pot boiling over on to your landlady's carpet, and no water to mop up any of it nearer than the bathroom at the other end of the landing. It is cooking at floor level, in a hurry, with nowhere to put the salad but the washing-up bowl, which in any case is full of socks.

However, with imagination, common sense, and a great deal of newspaper, all this can be surmounted; and excellent meals can be cooked without fuss even in the daintiest of lodgings.

I say 'the daintiest', for it is a sad fact that the better the room itself and the house in which it is found, the worse the cooking problem tends to be. In a large squalid rooming house, where the landlord calls only to collect the rent and where the cleaning, if any, is done by an indifferent slut with no standards to maintain, adventurous cooking is perfectly possible. If you find the sink filled with someone else's filthy crocks you can heave them out on to the floor without fear of a come-back. If you fill the whole house with the smell of burning onions you will be cursed but not evicted; and nothing will look much worse whatever you spill on it.

But in a respectable house you have much more to worry about. Often you are not really supposed to be cooking at all (it is a common fallacy among the better class of landladies that one can exist entirely on tea, biscuits, and good books, without the need for food, beer, the wireless, or the companionship of the opposite sex). At the slightest crash your landlady will come tittupping out of her sitting-room to worry about the effect you are having on her nice furniture. If you want to peel onions under running water, you will probably have to peel them in your bath; and there will be nobody from whom you can borrow salt or a corkscrew in moments of emergency.

But plenty of our troubles are of our own making. So many of us go into bedsitters, at least in the first instance, with the attitude of 'me all alone in my little room with my little pan and my little spoon' – and small pans, of course, make things ten times harder when you have only the one ring on which to cook everything you want to eat. Much better to think 'me with my enormous appetite and my huge stewpan'. One is also, unfortunately, apt to retain with fondness the bent knife, dented tin plate, and wonky-handled mug that one took to one's first Guide or Scout camp. The more restricted you are for space, the fewer implements you have, the more important it is to have the right ones – and that means tools that are big enough, thick enough, or sharp enough, according to their kind.

Knowing *what* to cook can be as big a headache as knowing how to cook it. I do not merely mean that life holds more than tinned dog-food and processed peas; but that it is hard to find recipes that are simple enough for beginners and yet suitable for a gas ring. Most of the cookery books and articles written for rabbits ('brides' is the polite term) begin with Basic English Cookery – and a great deal of basic English cookery is totally unsuited to bedsitters. To start with, a lot of it is simple without being particularly easy; and the worst of it – boiled parsnips, semolina pudding, stewed rhubarb – is abominably dull. (Why brides should be encouraged to produce this stuff I do not know: I can think of few better ways of heading for a speedy divorce.)

But a more important point is that the very *type* of cooking is all wrong for a gas ring. When we think of English cooking at its best, we instinctively think of vast nineteenth-century ranges, the huge oven barely containing the enormous sirloin; and of a gnarled retainer tottering in from the kitchen garden with soil-fresh vegetables. The principles of English cooking demand that first-class food should be cooked as simply as possible, and that a number of different foods should be cooked separately and served together. This is impossible on a gas ring. Indeed, bedsitter people have far more natural kinship with nomads brewing up in the desert over a small fire of camel dung, or impoverished Italian peasants eking out three shrimps and a lump of cheese with half a cartload of spaghetti.

The first thing a bedsitter cook must do is to abandon the notion of 'meat and two veg', in favour of the idea of a simmering cauldron. Meat, yes; vegetables, certainly – though it might be one or it might be four – but meat and vegetables deliberately chosen to be cooked together, so that the dish is all the better for one food sharing its flavours with another. And that brings us, inevitably, to the casserole.

## OUT OF THE FRYING PAN INTO THE CASSEROLE

A French politician representing a somewhat backward district in Africa was some time ago found to have been eaten by his constituents. The journalist who discovered this used the phrase: '*Je crois qu'il a passé par la casserole*' (I think he ended up in a casserole). Clearly the Africans knew what they were about. For making a delicious meal out of tough and intractable material, the casserole has no rival; and though, traditionally, most casseroles are oven dishes, all but the ones needing a crusty top can very well be done on a gas ring over an asbestos mat.

There is much to recommend casserole cookery. It is far the best way of cooking a number of different things together, as one must on a gas ring; the only smells it gives off are pleasant ones, and even those not for long; it is just as good – in some cases even better – if you heat it up the next day, so that you can make enough for two meals at a time. And, most important, there is a wide margin of error. If you fry a thing for five minutes too long, the chances are it will go up in flames; but with a casserole ten minutes or a few herbs one way or the other do not make such a great deal of difference. You get all the work over at the beginning, so that if you are expecting company or have other things to do, you can get on with other preparations and leave it quietly simmering; by and large, it is the easiest way to first-class results that I know.

It has, of course, the disadvantage of being slow. I quite realize that anyone coming in from an office is not going to settle down to a two hours' wait for supper (though not all dishes based on the casserole principle necessarily take *very* long – fish casseroles, for example, are quite quick). But there are always the week-ends, and there's a great deal to be said for cooking two meals one evening and then being able to come straight in the next and do nothing but heat the casserole up. Try to get into the habit of having a delicious potful simmering gently away; it takes so little gas (as little as possible) that coins in the meter need not be an added worry; and once you have grasped the principle you will, I am sure, prefer it to the everlasting fry, fry, fry.

## THE POTATO-SHAPED SPACE

Most of us have a potato-shaped space inside that must be filled at every meal, if not by potatoes, then by something equally filling – rice, bread, spaghetti, macaroni, and so on. This is a big problem for people coming hungrily home; for this is the part of the meal that often takes longest to cook, and it is often difficult to work in the cooking of potatoes or rice with other things. Where I could, I have tried to include instructions for adding potatoes or rice even to dishes in which they do not figure by nature; but anyone who cares greatly about speed would do well either to get into the habit of eating bread with a meal instead, or of cooking several days' supply of potatoes at a time (keeping them covered in the meantime) and just heating up a few in each new dish. Rice, too, will heat up all right with a little extra water, though if it stands for more than a day there will be some bits that have gone brittle and should be thrown out. By the same token, those who (rightly) care about eating green vegetables every day should get into the way of eating separate salads with their meals: that way, they may avoid having to cook an extra vegetable every time they feel they are running short on essential vitamins.

## STACKING

I am not much in favour of this business of trying to stack one food above another until you have a complete vertical meal. For one thing, you are always wanting to peer into layer one just when layer three should not be disturbed; for another, the whole leaning tower so often crashes violently to the floor. And it is a method which can produce some uncommonly dreary meals; I need only quote from one book that recommended this meal to the young and economical housewife: Boiled suet steak pudding, steamed potatoes, steamed parsnips, steamed semolina.

However, if you have a bowl which fits over your saucepan, there are some safe doubles that are worth trying. (1) Scrambled egg cooked over any vegetable, e.g. potatoes. The eggs are actually the nicer for this. (2) Any tin warmed up over cooking rice or potatoes saves you five minutes or so. (3) You can often keep something warm, or heat a few plates, over a meal that is cooking – and that *is* worth doing.

## TIMING

Knowing that people who live alone rarely start to cook until they are hungry, and that time (especially on weekdays) is of the essence, I have added to each recipe a rough guide to the time it will take. I have tried not to assume, as so many Lightning Cooks seem to do, that at the beginning of the recipe you are waiting in running shorts with everything round you, stop watch in hand and ready to set a world record. I am merely taking it that once you have started you will proceed with all deliberate speed – though of course I have not allowed for such things as the time it takes you to find the salt in the suitcase under the bed. Any recipe may take a little longer the first time, while you are still feeling your way.

One word of warning: if something is to taste delicious simply because it is cooked very, very slowly, you may ruin everything by turning up the gas and trying to hurry it. This applies to all slow casseroles and to everything in which an egg has to change its nature (e.g. scrambled egg, zabaione, custard) or in which two flavours (e.g. bacon and a vegetable) are supposed to have a chance to get together.

## THE WATER PROBLEM

No one who cooks in a real kitchen can imagine the unbelievable inconvenience of having no tap near the cooking. Nothing can be washed, swabbed, diluted, strained, or extinguished without first making that trip to the water-hole down the corridor. There are three things that help:

(1) Always have a damp cloth in the room with you to wipe the flour off your hands or the splashes off the walls.

(2) If you are going to be using water in the actual cooking, have a jug of the precious liquid standing by. It saves a lot of time.

(3) If by any chance you have to buy your own waste-paper basket, buy a plastic bucket instead. That way, you

can empty out dregs or even cooking water without having to leave the room.

## NEWSPAPER

You cannot do without it. It is your work-surface, your floor-covering, your splash-mat round the gas ring itself; it is the only way you can stop the coffee grounds falling through the slats of a wicker waste basket, and the neatest way to bundle up the débris for getting it out of the room. The nicer your room, the more newspaper you must spread around.

## ARRANGEMENT

Unless you are not supposed to be cooking in your bedsitter at all, you can save yourself a lot of trouble by deciding that one corner of the room is to be wholly given over to food. College girls who hide their cosmetics in their desks usually look as if they didn't bother about their faces; by the same token, if you care about food, don't hide it.

If you can find an offcut of Formica or Warerite at a hardware shop for a shilling or two, and put it down beside the gas ring and so have somewhere to put pans and forks when they are hot and dirty, you will simplify your life enormously. Similarly, a few pegs to hang things on – *any* things: fish slice, saucepan, onions, dish cloth – will keep the pressure off your cardboard box. Better a soap box of food by the gas ring than a fancy cupboard at the other side of the room. Localize the mess.

## SMELLS

Almost the worst problem of all – and there are no foolproof answers. However, it helps if you open the window when you start to cook, and not just when the stench becomes overpowering; if you cook all vegetables with a lid on (some say it spoils the colour – I'm not convinced, and never mind, anyway) and put a chunk of stale bread in with them. It helps if you start your casseroles (so many of which need an onion) in a heavy saucepan with a lid on, rather than in an open frying pan; and, when possible, if you *keep* the lid on something smelly until you can either park it on the window-sill to steam off for a minute or two or, trot down the corridor with it to the sink. It helps if you throw out things the moment you think they are going bad, rather than waiting till there's no doubt about it. It helps if you keep your frying pan clean: it's the little bits left over from last time that are most apt to burn and make a smell. It helps, too, to wipe off anything you spill on the gas ring, rather than let it burn off by degrees.

Some believe in chlorophyll; some don't. I cannot resist the chance to quote here the rhyme:

> *The stinking goat on yonder hill*
> *Feeds all day long on chlorophyll.*

It helps to sleep with a clothes-peg on your nose.

## KEEPING IT WITHIN LIMITS

'The whale is not a table fish,' said Belloc. I have given recipes only for food which will be cut into reasonably-sized pieces for you in the shop. The scene at St Trinian's where the Head discovers them roasting an ox whole in the dorm is as nothing to the scene that would ensue if your landlady found you trussing a hare all over her best carpet.

## EQUIPMENT

A good many cookery books start out by requiring a vast battery of equipment without which the simplest dish is doomed to failure. (I always burst into tears when I get to the bit about the little porcelain ramekins.) But here it is not a question of the *best* possible tools, but the *fewest*. You probably cannot afford elaborate equipment, and you certainly have no room for it: but the *right* simple tools will stop you longing for the other, complicated ones.

These are the things you should aim to have:

*A really sharp knife.* If the knife is to take the place of a mincer, a chopper, a grater, and kitchen scissors, it *must* be sharp. All those awful things you have to do to meat take half the time if the knife really cuts.

*A piece of wood.* It could be the back of the bread-board, or the underside of a wooden tray, or a simple plank bought for a shilling or so from a hardware shop. It will save you endless misery and mess, and speed your cooking immensely, as a chopping board for everything.

*A decent pan.* If you are to cook all your food in one pot, if it is to simmer deliciously for hours or heat attractively in a few minutes, if you are to fry in it with a lid on to prevent smells, it must be a good, big, heavy pan that will not burn every time you take your eye off it. I am not just being finicky: this is the first requirement.

*A frying pan.* Get a BIG one.

If you can manage to buy what they call a sauteuse, which is a cross between a small frying pan and a heavy saucepan, that would do beautifully for both of these. And if, in spite of all I say, you *will not* get yourself a decent saucepan, you can make quite a few of the casserole-type dishes by using an earthenware pot for the second stage (see under casseroles on page 15).

*A little saucepan* is needed for sauces, heating up cans, boiling and scrambling eggs, and so on.

*A bowl,* to be by turns a salad bowl, a pudding basin, a storage bowl, and a cooking bowl. One that will sit firmly over the top of one of your pans is twice as useful as one that won't; so it should be pottery, not plastic.

*A fish-slice* for getting things out of the frying pan.

*A tin-opener* that can work without covering the whole room in blood.

*A jug* (optional) in which you can make coffee or tea, or cook kippers, and which is handy for water and milk.

*An egg-beater* (optional) only costs about 70p; and though you *can* beat an egg white on a plate with a knife, it takes about ten minutes to do it.

An *asbestos mat* – or even two.

*A wooden spoon* saves a lot of wear on the nerves in the long run.

And that is all. You don't absolutely need a kettle: you can heat water in a saucepan if you must. Garlic squeezers, Mouli graters, potato peelers, and things for taking stones out of horses' hooves are a delight; but they take up space and cost money. You can manage without.

## STORES

If you are inclined to greet the mention of a store cupboard with a hollow laugh, let me hasten to explain that I am only talking about the cardboard box, lidless suitcase, or bedside cupboard where you normally keep your food: none of this will take up much room. But you have to keep *some* things in store – even a boiled egg would be ruinously expensive if you bought a new packet of salt every time – and they might as well be the right things.

This lot should see you through almost all the recipes in the book, leaving you to buy only the actual food involved, not a whole lot of extra bits.

*Salt*, *pepper*, and *mustard*; preferably French mustard. You can buy it in a tube, though the jar keeps well too.

A carton of *mixed herbs* and a bunch of *bay leaves*. (See section on herbs and seasonings, page 23.)

*Oil* in a bottle (or some sorts of olive oil in a can). *Olive oil* is nice, but expensive. *Groundnut oil* is flavourless, odourless, dirt cheap, and less messy than lard.

*Vinegar*; wine vinegar for choice.

*Lemon juice* in a plastic lemon is far less trouble than buying a lemon each time, and lasts for ages.

*Tomato paste.* Buy it in a tube to save waste.

*Meat* or *yeast extract.* A bottle is more economical than cubes.

*Garlic* (if you like it). A miniature tin of *ground garlic* saves trouble.

*Flour* (plain).

*Sugar.* Granulated is cheapest.

*Rice.* Always buy long-grain curry rice.

*Grated cheese* in a packet (cheaper), or a little tin (easier).

*Spices* suggested: *paprika*; *curry powder*; *chilli powder*; *cinnamon* or *ginger*. (See below on herbs and seasonings.)

If this seems too much to keep around, it may interest you to know that all that lot, plus a bottle of milk, a tin of coffee, a butter dish, a packet of teabags, a pot of jam, a pound of onions, three tomatoes, six eggs, and a packet of instant potato all fit quite easily on to one medium-sized tray.

## HERBS AND SEASONINGS

These are absolutely essential to good food, and anyone who already knows something about it may be disappointed that I have stuck to recommending mixed herbs in most of these recipes, instead of selecting the best herb to go with a particular dish. My defence is that bedsitter people have neither the space nor the money to indulge in a really comprehensive array of herbs, and that if they see rosemary on one page, thyme on the next, basil on the third, and so on, they will simply leave them out altogether; whereas if they realize that mixed herbs are wanted over and over again, they may actually buy some. Moreover, herbs lose their freshness only too quickly, and it is better to have a quick turnover in mixed herbs (which is only the poor man's *bouquet garni*, after all) than to have rows of different herbs gradually turning to hay on the bedsit windowsill.

Spices are another matter, since they do not go off; here it is simply a question of whether you like spiced food or not. I have tried for the sake of economy to suggest the same spice several times, rather than a different one on every page: those which crop up most are chilli powder (a great enlivener of indifferent meat), paprika, curry powder; ginger is not mentioned very often, but you can use a lot if you eat it on melon; cinnamon, mentioned only twice, can also be used to make cinnamon toast.

A word on ground vegetable seasonings. If you like to have celery, shallots, garlic, and onion by you in semi-permanent form (and why not), do buy the pure powder in tins rather than garlic salt, celery salt, etc. Otherwise you will find you easily make your food too salty.

## KEEPING FOOD IN A BEDSITTER

*Meat.* Meat goes off very quickly in hot weather, and liver and kidneys even faster. Take the wrapping paper off meat as soon as you get it home – the paper often begins to smell awful long before the meat itself would really be bad. And get into the habit of dusting it with salt, which does help a little. But there is a better way – and that is:

*Marinade – the Poor Man's Fridge.* A marinade is a mixture of vinegar (or wine), oil, herbs, salt, pepper, and maybe a bit of chopped onion. Meat soaked in this keeps much better than meat left exposed to the air, and it will also be more tender. The idea is that the acid in the vinegar breaks down the fibres, the oil makes it all juicier, and the herbs and seasonings give it flavour. Meat will not keep for ever this way, but even in hot weather lamb chops thrown into a marinade at, say, lunch-time on Saturday will still be perfectly all right on Sunday evening, and in cool weather they will keep for several days. You can use the same mixture for another meat, for up to five days at least. Nor need you make enough actually to cover the meat; dip it in, both sides, and turn it occasionally.

*Butter and Fats.* You can buy special butter dishes of earthenware that sit in water and help to keep butter cool by the effect of evaporation; a cheap way of doing the same thing is to stand the butter in its paper in a saucer of water, under an upturned and frequently watered flower pot. In heat waves, use margarine – but remember that it is not much good for frying. *Don't* use those greasy little plastic boxes so often seen around bedsitters. They don't help to preserve the fat, and there is a great tendency among their possessors to put in fresh butter without entirely cleaning out the old lot: with rancid results.

*Frozen Food and Ice-Cream.* These will not keep frozen very long, and unless you have a wide-mouthed thermos there are only two things you can do to prolong their coldness: (1) Choose the packet from the bottom of the freezer; (2) remember that insulation for cold is the same as insulation for heat. If you want to keep an ice-cream cold, wrap it in a blanket.

The coldest place in a bedsitter is very often under the bed. By all means keep food there, in a suitable box; though you had better find a way of reminding yourself of its presence before it reminds you.

## QUANTITIES

One man's meat is another man's cocktail sausage. If you are not sure just how filling a dish is going to be, check down the list of the things that are in it: even the flour in a sauce will nourish you somewhat. The recipes in the 'Cooking to Stay Alive' section are mostly for one person, and where I have put 'two helpings' the reason is that the dish either takes too long or is rather too much trouble to be worth while making for yourself for just one meal. There are also some dishes which are too much fuss to make for yourself, which are too messy or too smelly to cook for proper visitors, but which are none the less delicious to eat. These are for you to cook with another bedsitite like yourself.

In the puddings section, most are for two or four people; in the 'Cooking to Impress' section, recipes are for two or four as stated.

## MEASUREMENTS

I have tried to use as measures only things that you would have by you anyway, such as spoons. The only things for which I have given the quantities in pounds and ounces are the things you would buy in that way, such as meat and mushrooms.

Spoon measures are rounded – not flat, but not heaped as high as they will go.

A cup means a fairly large cup, or a breakfast cup not absolutely full. A small cup is the dainty teacup size.

Pints and half pints can be measured in a clean milk bottle.

For those who like to know where they stand:

2 teaspoons = 1 dessertspoon; 2 dessertspoons = 1 tablespoon.

 1 flat tablespoon = half a rounded tablespoon
 4 rounded tablespoons (or 8 flat) = 1 small cup
 6 rounded tablespoons (or 12 flat) = 1 full cup
 1 tablespoon of a liquid is the same as 1 flat tablespoon
 6 tablespoons of a liquid = $\frac{1}{4}$ pint
 1 cup flour = $\frac{1}{4}$ lb. flour
 1 small cup sugar = $\frac{1}{4}$ lb. sugar

✳✳✳✳✳✳✳✳✳✳✳✳✳✳✳✳✳✳✳✳✳✳✳✳

## CHAPTER 2
# *Beginner's Index*

METHODS: EXPLANATIONS: HOW MUCH TO
BUY: HOW TO PREPARE: STANDARD COOKING
TIMES

APPLES: Cooking apples are large, green, and cheap; 1 lb. is
an ample helping for one or a small helping for two. Stew
gently in a little water with a tablespoon of sugar, or more,
for 15–20 mins., depending on the kind of apples. Tinned
apple purée can be bought to save time; the baby-food tins
are the right size for one.

ARTICHOKE, GLOBE: This looks like a cross between a
pineapple and a green fir cone. One is usually enough
for each person. Cook in boiling water with lid on until
a leaf pulls out easily; eat cold with a French dressing
(page 102) with a teaspoon of extra vinegar in it. You
eat it by pulling out a leaf, dipping it in the sauce, and
biting off the tender bit at the end. There is a soft bit at
the bottom of the crown to eat too, but you don't eat the
whiskers.

ARTICHOKE, JERUSALEM: This looks like an old knobbly
potato. Peel and boil with lid on, as if it was a potato.
Allow about 1 lb. for one; 20 mins. to boil.

AUBERGINE (or EGGPLANT): A dark purple bulbous vegetable that tastes delicious. Allow one good-sized aubergine
per person; don't choose wrinkled ones. Cheapest in the
autumn. Needs no peeling if used in casseroles. Goes
brown like an apple, so do not peel before you need it.
Good fried; you can cut them up, salt them, and dry them
before you fry. Takes 10 mins. to fry over gentle heat, cut
in strips.

BABY MARROWS: see COURGETTES.

BACON: Streaky is cheaper than back, which is the kind with the lean all in one piece. Buy it in a vacuum pack, and it will keep till you need it – a week at least, often more (see page 54.)

BATTER: A mixture of flour, milk, and egg (or oil, for Scampi); for pancakes or fritters. (See 'Pancakes and Fritters', page 114.)

BAY LEAVES: Buy them dried, and use them in small quantities in casseroles and when cooking rice. Half a leaf is enough in most dishes for one.

BEANS, BROAD: If you buy them in the pod, you need nearly 1 lb. for each person; be sure to remove the little half-moon on the edge of each bean. They take 10–15 mins. to cook in boiling salted water, depending on size. Good frozen.

BEANS, FRENCH: The long green ones. If you buy them fresh, $\frac{1}{4}$ lb. is enough for one. Remove top and tip, and pull off any long string down the side of old ones. They are good eaten cooked and cold, with French dressing put on while they are still warm. Not very good in tins, except expensive French or Italian ones. 15 mins. in boiling water with lid on.

BEANS, HARICOT: Usually this means small white dried beans. Soak overnight, and follow a recipe as to quantity.

BEEF: See page 79. Buy $\frac{1}{4}$ lb. for one person. (See also under FRYING.)

BEER: See under WINE.

BEETROOT: Best bought ready cooked, but can be reheated, as well as eaten cold. Just remove the roughened outside. A medium-size beetroot is enough for one; smaller if you want it just in a salad.

BISCUITS: Do not keep in the same tin as cake or they will go soft.

BRAISING: This means cooking something slowly in a pan, with the lid on, in a little fat; or sometimes in a very little other liquid, such as vegetable stock. It is sort of slow, enclosed frying.

BREAD: Keep it in a Polythene bag.

BREADCRUMBS: Breadcrumbs are a bore in a bedsitter, but sometimes one must have them. There are four ways of getting them:

(1) Buy them. Some bought breadcrumbs are an alarming shade of orange and suitable only for fish; others are quieter in tone and will do for Wiener Schnitzel, fried chicken, etc. Bought breadcrumbs are not very suitable for the kind of pudding where you will eat them as they are, without further cooking.

(2) Dry slices of bread in front of the fire until they are hard; wrap up in newspaper, and first bang then roll the parcel until it is a parcel of crumbs.

(3) If you have a grater, you can grate a chunk of bread to make soft crumbs; but these are no good for frying.

(4) Get some housewife who hates to waste crusts to give you some of her crumbs.

BROWNING FLOUR: This is too dangerous. Expert cookery books recommend giving colour to casseroles by cooking the flour at the beginning until it is coloured brown; but one false move and it burns, goes grey, and the dish is ruined in taste as well as appearance.

BROWNING IN FAT: At the beginning of many meat dishes you fry the meat quickly on all sides to seal in the juices. After this the meat can go on cooking at a lower temperature. Always worth doing.

BRUSSELS SPROUTS: Take off outer withered-looking leaves. Cut a small cross in the base of each sprout. Allow about $\frac{1}{2}$ lb. if you like a lot of them; and cook in boiling salted water 15 mins. with lid on.

BUTTER: Salted butter keeps slightly better than unsalted. (See page 24.)

CABBAGE: Wash carefully; make cuts in thick stalk part; remove messy outer leaves; chop. Allow $\frac{1}{4}$ lb. cabbage for one (except where it is the basis for a full dish, where see recipe); cook in a *very little* boiling salted water 10–15 mins. with the lid on and a lump of bread in it to help control the smell. (Red cabbage is the same, but takes longer to cook.)

CARROTS: Scrape new ones; peel old ones. Slice in rings or in long slices. Allow about ¼ lb. per person. Cook in boiling salted water 15–20 mins. Also good grated in salads.

CASSEROLE: See page 15 for arguments in favour. The standard method for casseroles is: first turn the meat in hot fat for a minute or two on all sides to seal in juices; remove from pan and fry onions for a few minutes; stir flour into fat *off the gas* if you are using flour; add vegetables and liquid, and put back meat. (You can dip the meat in flour instead of adding the flour separately, if you like.) If you have a heavy pan, do all the cooking in the same pan. If not, start off in a frying pan, and when you come to putting in the vegetables, etc., put it all into an earthenware casserole and stand it over an asbestos mat. *Do not put an earthenware casserole on to a direct flame.* Casseroles should cook as slowly as possible.

CAULIFLOWER: A whole, very small cauliflower is a full meal for one; half a small one is more than enough if it is an accompanying vegetable (see page 63). Cauliflower takes 15 mins. in boiling salted water with lid on; cut stalks small if you plan to eat them, as they take longer.

CELERY: At its best raw (in salads, or alone). Can also be cooked in boiling salted water 15 mins. with lid on. Cut off hub at bottom, leafage at top. Tinned celery tastes good, and cut pieces are as good as whole heads. A small head per person is enough when it is a separate vegetable.

CHICKEN: See page 92. Boiling chicken pieces take 1–3 hrs, depending on their age. (See also under FRYING.)

CHICKEN LIVERS: Can be bought separately. Pick over carefully and remove any odd-looking bits; wash. Allow $\frac{1}{4}$ lb. or less, per person, depending on the dish. They go leathery if over-cooked. (See also under FRYING.)

CHICORY: Buy one white head of it per person; do not unwrap, just cut off hub and any bruised tips. Either cut in chunks and eat as a salad, or boil 15 mins. with lid on. If you dislike the bitter taste, bring water to boil with chicory in it, throw out the water and start again with fresh.

CHILLI: A hot spice useful in Mexican types of food; very strong; half a teaspoonful spices 1 lb. of meat.

CIDER: See under WINE.

CINNAMON: A spice used in cooking sweet dishes, also in making Cinnamon Toast. Keeps indefinitely.

CLOVES: A spice used with apples, and in many stews and casseroles. One clove will flavour 1 lb. apples.

COD: Usually comes either in steaks (with a bit of bone in the middle) or in fillets. You need one steak, one large fillet, or two little ones, per person. Takes 10–15 mins. of *gentle* simmering to cook. Has a black skin which can be removed easily afterwards. A frozen packet is a generous helping for one. (See also under FRYING.)

COFFEE: See page 130.

CORNFLOUR: Used in sauces and (more commonly) for making puddings; especially for cold ones which set solid. (Gelatine also does this, and takes no time to cook.) As it is always hard to get anything with cornflour in it to taste of anything except cornflour, I have only used it in about two recipes. You must always cook it for 10 mins. to try to remove that taste.

COURGETTES: Small Continental marrows. Can be gently stewed in oil for 15–30 mins. Allow $\frac{1}{4}$–$\frac{1}{2}$ lb. per person.

CREAM: Cream is sold in bottles, and in cartons which cost relatively more. If you want to beat cream stiff, you must use double cream – single cream won't whip – but you can stretch it somewhat with top-of-the-milk added in small quantities when it begins to stiffen. Permanently bottled cream has a slight taste: it is all right in cooking but not so good in cold sweet dishes. Cream should be added to hot dishes only shortly before eating.

CREAM, SOUR: Can be bought in cartons; or you can sour some ordinary cream by adding a few drops of vinegar or lemon juice. Sour milk or yoghourt is a good substitute – but not advanced sour milk that is all whey and green mould.

CUCUMBER: A quarter of a cucumber is enough for one in a salad. No need to peel it for salads – the food value, such as it is, is in the skin. Slice as thin as possible for use in salads; but for cooking, peel and cut into chunks.

CURRY: See page 100. Curry powder keeps indefinitely.

CUSTARD: A mixture of eggs and milk used for pouring over fruit, or allowed to get cold and set. Custard powder has instructions on the packet. (For Egg Custard, see page 121.)

DEVILLED: Means mixed with a sauce or with flavourings that are 'hot' in the sense that curry is hot – mustard, pickles, sometimes vinegar and pepper, etc. There are several recipes for devilled food. (See pages 52, 134.)

DUBLIN BAY PRAWNS: See under SCAMPI.

EGGS: The different methods of cooking eggs are described on page 48, for poaching, frying, boiling, scrambling, and on pages 59–63, for omelettes, egg dishes, etc. EGG WHITES AND YOLKS: (1) *To separate.* Break egg neatly in the middle; hold one half upright with the yolk in it while the white pours off into a bowl or cup beneath; pass the yolk back and forth between the two half egg-shells, until no white remains. Remember to have two receptacles ready before you start – to save wandering round the room with an egg yolk looking for somewhere to put it. (2) *To keep.* Whites will keep for a week if covered; yolks only for a day or two. If unbroken, cover the yolk(s) with water. (3) *Beating egg whites.* If you have no beater, you can beat one or two whites on a plate with a knife, which is less wearying than trying to beat them in a cup with a fork, but takes 10 mins. Mixing beaten egg whites: do it very gently with a fork, trying as far as possible not to smash down the fluffiness. EGG WHITES WILL NOT STAY BEATEN LONG. BEAT JUST BEFORE YOU NEED THEM. (4) *Cooking egg yolks*. These have a tendency to curdle, so always cook them *very* gently; if possible over a pan of water, rather than directly on the heat. Yolks can be added to almost any sauce or mixed dish to enrich it, but it *must not* be boiled after the yolk is in.

FLOUR. Plain flour is used for all the recipes in this book. Flour in cooking must always cook for 10 mins. or more, to remove the taste of raw starch, which can ruin any dish. Never add flour to any dry mixture over a very hot flame – it may burn, and will taste dreadful if it does.

FRENCH DRESSING: See page 102. Add it to solid foods, such as tomato, potato, and mushroom, an hour or so before you eat it; add to leaf salads, such as lettuce, watercress, only just before eating.

FRITTERS: See page 116.

FROZEN FOOD: Better than tinned from the health point of view, and not always more expensive: remember you are not paying, by the pound, for the bits that you throw away – peeling, bones, etc. – as you are with fresh food. *To unfreeze*: Fruit must simply sit in the warm room until it is unfrozen; taking it out of its packet speeds things up. Fish can be unfrozen under the cold tap (if you hold it under the hot tap, little bits will start to cook in the warm water and flake off). Vegetables need not be unfrozen before cooking, unless you are adding them to a hot casserole.

FRYING: I have used the word frying in this book for a good many processes which should by rights have more precise names – browning, sautéing, and so on – because everyone knows what frying means. Oil, or a mixture of oil and butter, is the best fat for frying; lard or dripping will do, but many lards have a 'taste' which affects foods cooked in them. Margarine won't fry properly unless you add a little oil.

*Deep fat frying*: The hotter the fat the better; but you don't want it to catch fire, so compromise and put in food as soon as fat stops bubbling. Fat should not come farther up the pan than 2½ ins. from the top, or it may bubble over. Chips take about 6 minutes; pieces of fish about 5; fritters about 4. Any food is done when it is a deep golden brown. A frying basket is useful and cheap, but not essential.

*Shallow fat frying*: The following table gives the times for shallow fat frying. Where the heat of fat is not given, see the appropriate section in this Index.

| | |
|---|---|
| Bacon | 3 mins. each side, medium heat |
| Beef steak (thin) | 3 mins. each side |
| (thick) | 5 mins. each side |
| (minute) | 1 min. each side |
| Chicken (in pieces) | 10 mins. or more each side in very hot fat |
| Chips (thin) | 10 mins. in hot fat |
| Chicken livers | 5 mins., gentle heat |
| Eggs | 4 mins., gentle heat |
| Fish (thin fillets) | 3 mins. each side, medium heat |
| (thick steaks) | 7 mins. each side, medium heat |
| Kidneys (halved) | 5 mins. each side, gentle heat |
| Lamb chops | 5–7 mins. each side in hot fat; or 10–13 mins. each side, gentle heat |
| Liver | 7–10 mins. each side, gentle heat |
| Mushrooms (chopped) | 6 mins. medium heat |
| Onions | 10 mins. in hot fat (browned) 15 mins. medium hot fat (golden) |
| Mutton chops | 8 mins. each side, medium heat |

| Pork chops | 12 mins. each side, medium heat |
| Veal (cutlets) | 5 mins. each side, medium heat |
| (escalopes) | 2 mins. each side, hot fat |
| Sausages | 10 mins. medium hot, turning often |

*(All fried meat and chicken is improved by being given one min. each side at the beginning on hotter flame than the rest of the frying.)*

GARLIC: Comes in a small onion-shaped bulb; each little section of it is a *clove* of garlic. Chop it up fine for adding to meat dishes. Garlic smells strongest when raw (e.g. when rubbed round a salad bowl). I suppose it is better not to use too much when looking forward to a romantic evening. My own view is rather that of my sister-in-law, who gave me a garlic squeezer with the words: 'If your friends don't like garlic, get some new friends.'

GELATINE: A tablespoon of unflavoured powdered gelatine usually sets a pint of liquid; but read what it says on the packet, as different brands sometimes vary. It is easier if you moisten the gelatine with a little water before you mix it in with the rest of the liquid. In hot weather, if you are in a hurry, use slightly more; in cold weather, when cooking for the following day, use slightly less.

GINGER (ground): Used in sweet dishes; also served with melon. Keeps indefinitely.

GRATER: If you are buying a grater, a rotary ('Mouli' mincer) one will stop you grating your fingers as well as the food.

GRATING: If you have no grater, you can still achieve grated cheese, chocolate, carrot, etc., by shaving little splinters off with a really sharp knife. For grated lemon peel, cut off very thin slivers of peel (with no white bits) and then chop them like parsley, holding the point firmly down in one hand while you bang the blade up and down with the other.

35

GRAVY: For your purposes, gravy is made by shaking a dessertspoon of flour into the fat or fatty liquid in which meat was cooked, adding a little water, going on stirring it until it thickens, and then allowing it to bubble gently for at least 5 mins. (*Don't* use gravy-browning in a bedsitter, as for some reason it is impossible to stop the stuff crawling out of the bottle and making brown rings everywhere.) Use a little meat extract if you think the thing needs pepping up – or let your sauces and gravies be pale but interesting, like a good poet, and nobody will complain. Gravy cubes are pretty well foolproof: follow instructions on packet. Bisto or gravy powder works OK.

HADDOCK: A cheerful orangey-yellow fish. $\frac{1}{2}$ lb. is a generous helping for one. Treat as for cod. Smoked haddock has an excellent taste, which survives freezing better than most flavours.

HAKE: $\frac{1}{2}$ lb. is a generous helping for one. Treat as for cod.

HEAT: The phrases I have used to describe the relative heat at which you cook your food describe four states of the gas ring.

*Lowest possible*: means as low as it will go without blowing out, plus one or even two asbestos mats.

*Gentle*: means a flame the size of a large pea.

*Medium flame*: less than $\frac{1}{2}$ in. high.

*High*: as high as it will go – and watch it.

HERBS: See page 23. Mixed herbs should be fresh; they improve most meat dishes. Allow $\frac{1}{4}$ teaspoon to composite dishes for one or two. (See also under MINT, PARSLEY, TARRAGON.)

HERRING: Two herrings make a good meal for one. Get the fishmonger to remove head and guts; or buy them frozen. You can also buy them ready cooked for salads. (See also under FRYING.)

KALE: Treat like cabbage.

KIDNEYS: See page 57 and also under FRYING.

KIPPERS (simply herrings, smoked): Can be fried or cooked in a jug (see page 48). Allow one for breakfast, two for supper for one.

LAMB: See page 87 and also under FRYING.

LEEKS: Two large or three small leeks make a full helping for one – about 1 lb. Leeks manage to get an astonishing amount of grit into their innermost recesses, so must always be slit to the centre and the individual leaves parted for washing. They take just under 15 mins. to cook, and should be drained if possible. Good cooked, or cold as a salad (put the dressing on while they are still warm).

LENTILS (small red or large brown): ⅓ cup dried lentils for one; boil hard for ½ hour; no soaking needed (unless for those with specially delicate digestions).

LETTUCE: Cabbage lettuce is round and bushy, cos lettuce tall and flat-leaved. Lettuce must be washed. If you cannot drain it, wrap it in a cloth and swing it about. It will spatter the walls and ceiling slightly, but only with tiny harmless drops. Lettuce is good for you, but has less vitamins than watercress. Dressing should be added only at the last minute.

LIVER: See page 56 and also under FRYING.

MACARONI: Buy by the pound. Keeps indefinitely. (See page 74.)

MACKEREL: A good cheap fish. One mackerel for one person. Get the fishmonger to clean it for you.

MARGARINE: Keeps longer than butter in hot weather. Mix with a little oil for frying, or it will fizzle away to nothing.

MARINADE: A way of tenderizing and preserving meat (see page 24). Make as for French dressing – i.e. 1 part vinegar, 2 parts oil, herbs, mustard, salt, pepper, chopped onion (optional). You can increase the proportion of vinegar. Mix thoroughly; dip meat in it both sides; turn meat from time to time. Keeps meat for several days.

MEAT: See under different headings: BEEF, VEAL, MUTTON, etc.

MEAT or YEAST EXTRACT: Bovril, Oxo, Marmite, and so
forth will dissolve all right in hot water. The water does
not have to be boiling. Usual proportions are 1 teaspoon
to a cup of water, both for cooking and drinking. It is
cheaper to buy it in bottles than cubes.

MILK: To stop milk going off in really hot weather, scald it;
i.e. bring it to boiling point. It doesn't taste so good, but
then neither does sour milk, come to that. Always cook
milk with the lid off. Milk for coffee can be heated but
should never be boiled. If you heat milk often (for cocoa,
etc.) and it is *always* boiling over, you can buy a thing
called a milk-saver – a glass disc which allows milk to
bubble gently without actually flooding the floor.

MINT: Nice in salads, improves peas and potatoes if a sprig
is cooked with them. Mint sauce is simply chopped fresh
mint, vinegar, and sugar in proportions to suit your
preference. Mint can be bought in sprigs and will keep in
water like a flower, sometimes for weeks.

MUSHROOMS: Should always be washed, almost never need
peeling. Peel only the really grimy-looking ones. Small
white round-looking or 'button' mushrooms can be
sliced with their stalks; old wood mushrooms should
have their stalks removed, but the stalks are quite edible;
they just need finer chopping. Large black wood mushrooms will colour a whole dish black, but taste superb.
Mushrooms take 6 mins. to fry gently and are also good
uncooked in salads.

MUTTON: See under 'Lamb and Mutton', page 87; see also
under FRYING.

OIL: Probably the best thing for frying in a bedsitter. It is
less expensive than butter, less smelly and messy than lard,
and has either a better flavour or none at all. *Olive Oil* is
not cheap, but is excellent in salad dressing and in all
Mediterranean dishes (e.g. Ratatouille, Frying Pan Pizza)
where an authentic taste is important. *Groundnut Oil* is
extremely cheap, and can be used for frying or in salad

dressings; it is completely neutral, has no flavour good or bad. Oil does not go bad.

ONIONS: Small ones are stronger, larger ones milder. Always useful to keep by you, even if you keep them in a box because of the faint smell that some of them give off. Peel under a tap if you can; fry with a lid on if you can. Can be eaten boiled (takes 15–20 mins., allow four per person) and are the basic vegetable in dozens of casseroles. (See also under FRYING.) SPRING ONIONS are eaten raw in salads; you eat the white part, cut off the hard hub at the bottom and the greens at the top, and remove outer thin skin if it looks dirty. (You will not smell your sweetest after eating these.)

PANCAKES: See page 114.

PAPRIKA: A mild peppery spice used in Austro-Hungarian dishes like Goulash. It is quite unlike Chilli, except in appearance; one can use a dessertspoonful to 1 lb. of meat.

PARSLEY: Fresh parsley costs little, and will keep in water, like a flower, for a long time. It is good chopped finely and sprinkled on the top of plain fried meat, and it comes into an enormous number of composite dishes. Chop by holding point of knife firmly in one hand while you bang the blade up and down with the other. *Dried parsley* is not nearly so potent, and some have no faith in it at all; personally I think it is better than nothing, provided you use it in twice the quantity you would use if it was fresh.

PARSNIPS: $\frac{1}{2}$ lb. is enough for one. Peel thickly; cut in long thick strips; boil in salted water 20 mins. or longer, depending on age. Improved if then well mashed with plenty of butter and pepper – but they still taste of parsnip.

PEAS: It cannot be too widely known that '*processed*' *peas* are simply dried peas boiled up and coloured a lurid green before being put into the tin. Their food value is low.

*Garden peas* are all right; and *petits pois* are very good indeed – but, alas, more expensive. Frozen peas compare very well in price both with tinned peas and fresh. If you are buying fresh peas, get $\frac{1}{2}$–$\frac{3}{4}$ lb. per person. They take 8–12 mins. to boil, according to their size. (*Don't* boil them until khaki-coloured.) The dried peas you buy in a shiny packet cook fast and taste like frozen. (Split peas, yellow or green, are treated in the same way as lentils.)

PEPPERS, GREEN: See under PIMENTOES. These are sweet peppers and have nothing to do with pepper the seasoning.

PIGEONS: Some pigeons are just the right size for one. Cook as on page 136. Get the poulterer to remove guts, head, etc.

PILCHARDS: A good cheap tinned fish. Comes in a tomato sauce, which you can wash off under the tap if you want to use them in a creamy dish. Remove backbone, too.

PIMENTOES (or GREEN PEPPERS): These are a vegetable about the size of an apple, dark green (or red or yellow) and empty, except for a few seeds and a little white membrane, which you remove – through a hole in the top if you are going to stuff them. They have a strong, delightful flavour, and are cheap in the autumn; but even at other seasons you need only a very little to give flavour to a dish, and they weigh light. You can also eat them as a vegetable on their own – and they are delicious raw, either in green salad or alone and undressed.

PINEAPPLE: Fresh pineapple goes brown if left uncovered, and must not be used for trifles, etc. Tinned pineapple is good; chunks are cheapest and taste the same as rings – it's just a question of shape. Some savoury dishes contain pineapple.

PINEAPPLE JUICE: Cheaper in tins than in bottles.

PLAICE: A flat fish. Allow one per person, or two if small. You can ask the fishmonger to fillet it for you, but usually it is enough if he removes the head. Good frozen. (See also under FRYING.)

PORRIDGE: Buy the kind of oatmeal that has been beaten out flat and therefore needs no soaking. One cup per person is a good hefty serving. (See page 47.)

POTATOES: Allow ½ lb. per person, or two to three medium-sized potatoes. Take 20 mins. to boil from the moment you put on the water. Cook with lid on. Can be cooked un-peeled if they are clean, but if they are earthy the earth will mark the pan and it will take you longer to clean it than to peel the potatoes. You can buy *instant potato* (which makes up quickly into mashed, and is quite nice if you use lots of milk and butter; but it is a terribly expensive way to eat potatoes) and *tinned potatoes*. Tinned potatoes vary greatly, try different brands; most are quite good in salad. CHIPS are best fried in deep fat. The two things which make them nice are: (1) drying them before they go in the pan; (2) taking them out as soon as they begin to colour; draining them, and putting them back to finish at the last minute (you can do the first part hours before, if you like). MASHED are improved by adding butter and a little milk, and/or having an onion boiled with the potatoes and mashed up too. (See also under FRYING.)

PORK: See page 90; also under FRYING.

PRAWNS: See under SCAMPI:

RABBIT: Buy chopped-up pieces; two are a full meal for one. One will do if pieces are large. (See pages 82, 84 for cooking rabbit on one ring, page 137 for a way that needs two.) Soak in vinegar and water for an hour or two, if possible.

RHUBARB: Cut off the leaves and the hard bit at the bottom; do not peel. Cut in 3 or 4 in. pieces, put in enamel or earthenware pot (aluminium causes loss of colour and harsh flavour) with plenty of sugar or honey and a bit of lemon peel; add water to half-way up or less. Put on low gas and bring slowly to the boil. Don't keep it boiling; when it boils, turn off.

RICE: Always buy the long-grained type of rice: it has much less tendency to gum up in the pan. One-third cup raw rice is about right for one, unless it is the whole basis of a dish, in which case allow ½ cup. Rice will absorb about twice its own volume of liquid if cooked slowly; if you are cooking it fast, allow more, because evaporation will remove some as well. (See page 78 for one-ring ways with rice; page 133 for two-ring ways.) If available, 'Momento' instant rice (pour on boiling water and stand 15 mins.) is useful.

SAUCES: In this book most of the sauces are made as an essential stage in the making of a complete dish, rather than something to be added afterwards. However, the principle which is the foundation for a great many sauces and casseroles and other composite dishes is the same: for the sake of convenience rather than accuracy let us call it the *White Sauce Principle*.

| | |
|---|---|
| 1 teaspoon of butter | 1 cup (or a little less or a little |
| 1 dessertspoon of flour | more) of milk |

(The milk is often replaced by another liquid: stock, or the liquid from a tin.)

(1) Melt the butter in a saucepan over a gentle heat. (2) Shake in the flour, stirring hard. Off the heat altogether is safest. It will make a rather dry-looking mixture with the butter. (3) Stir in, gradually, over a low heat, the milk or other liquid. If lumps appear, stir hard, and as it is easier to stir out lumps while the sauce is still very thick, stir out all lumps before adding more liquid. (4) Go on stirring till it thickens; and then, unless the sauce is to cook for a longer time with other food, it *must* bubble gently for nearly 10 minutes, or it will taste, revoltingly, of raw starch.

TARTARE SAUCE: for fish, see page 170. MINT SAUCE: For lamb and mutton, see under MINT. CHOCOLATE SAUCE, see POIRES BELLE HÉLÈNE, page 119. SAUCE LYALL: for fish, see page 99.

SANDWICHES: See page 109 for cold sandwiches, page 112 for hot. Cold sandwiches can be made some hours before eating, if you wrap them in a Polythene bag or damp cloth.

SCALLOPS: A shellfish which comes in an attractive shell, the shell being useful for serving other things. One or two per person, depending on whether it is first course or main course. You eat the red part and the white part, but not the black beard, and you take it off its shell to cook.

SCAMPI (or DUBLIN BAY PRAWNS): Can be bought fresh or frozen, and are generally eaten either deep-fat fried in batter (see page 116) or gently fried in butter and sprinkled with parsley; or wrapped in a sauce. Expensive but delicious. Eight big prawns or one large frozen packet is a main course for two. Serve with lemon, and tartare sauce.

SIMMER: This means cooking something just *below* boiling point – only an occasional bubble should rise to the surface. In practice this is often hard to achieve on a gas ring, but keep the gas as low as possible and sit the pan on one or even two asbestos mats.

SOLE: Buy fresh or frozen. A large fillet or two small for each person. (See also under FRYING.)

SPAGHETTI: Buy in long packets. Allow 25 strands or more per helping. Keeps indefinitely. (See page 70.)

SPINACH: If you buy spinach fresh, you have to buy an armful to make one helping; and you must remove the stalk from each separate leaf. Allow $\frac{1}{2}$ lb. per person. Wash. Pack into large pan, with no water except what adheres from washing. Keep the lid down with a weight (e.g. a full tin of something) if necessary. Put on low gas. It cooks in 10 mins. (small leaf young spinach may take less). Drain off the dark juice. This method retains the fresh green colour as well as the vitamins. Frozen spinach is excellent, and tinned is definitely one of the better buys, especially as you can buy spinach purée, which is too much trouble to do from scratch in a bedsitter. The more butter you can mix into spinach, the nicer it is.

STEAK: See page 80. Allow $\frac{1}{4}$ lb. per person, and more if they have good appetites. Always make a few slits in the fat, to prevent it curling. (See also under FRYING.)

STOCK: With ordinary kitchen cookery, stock is the flavoured water which is left when you have boiled bones or vegetables or meat trimmings. It is used for enriching composite dishes and making soup. In most cases, you will not be bothering with this (the only exception is Lamb Pilaff, page 158), so use either a teaspoon of meat extract, or a soup cube dissolved in a cup of water; beef for all meat dishes, chicken for chicken dishes.

SWEDES: Allow $\frac{1}{2}$ lb. for one. Peel thickly and cut in slices or small chunks and boil with the lid on 20 mins., or longer if old. Mash with butter.

SWEETCORN: Can be bought fresh, but very good tinned or frozen. Sweetcorn grows on a 'cob', that is a husk, 4–8 in. long; Corn on the Cob (see page 70) means sweetcorn served on this husk. Allow one cob per head for a first course, and cook 15 mins. in boiling salted water with the lid on. Cooking longer makes it tougher.

TARRAGON: A very attractive herb, often used when cooking chicken.

TEA: See page 131. Allow two teaspoons to a pot from which you expect four large cups.

THICKENING A SAUCE: Put a dessertspoon of flour into a cup; mix to a smooth paste with a little of the water from saucepan; gradually add more, and pour back into pan. *Warning*: Never thicken a sauce just before serving. The flour must have at least 10 mins. to cook, or it will taste of raw starch. Adding an egg yolk just before serving also thickens a sauce – but it mustn't boil after that.

TINS: Once you have opened a tin, eat or remove the contents. Food left in tins is always said to go off.

TOMATOES: Need not be peeled for salads, and in casseroles only if you are expecting company. If left unpeeled, tomatoes will leave stray bits of skin floating about in the casserole on their own. The easiest way to skin tomatoes is to pour boiling or very hot water over them and let them stand for a minute or two; after that the skins will come off like gloves. Or you can turn a tomato on a fork round and round over a high gas; the effect is the same.

TOMATO PASTE OR PURÉE: Mostly made in Italy, this comes in tins of various sizes, and in tubes. Helps to soften meat; adds flavour to many dishes.

TRIPE: One of the cheapest foods there is; $\frac{1}{4}$–$\frac{1}{2}$ lb. per person. (See page 58.)

TURNIPS: Allow about $\frac{1}{2}$ lb. per person, or less if used in stews, etc. Peel thickly and cut in slices or thin chunks. Boil 20 mins. with lid on.

VEAL: See page 85 and also under FRYING.

VINEGAR: Used mainly in French dressing. Wine vinegar tastes better than malt vinegar.

WATERCRESS: A green salad vegetable, with leaves about the size of a sixpence – not to be confused with cress of the mustard-and-cress variety, which looks more like grass stalks. Wash thoroughly, as watercress is not fussy about where it grows. Has more vitamins than lettuce. Generally bought by the bunch. Makes a good garnish for fried meat – uncooked, of course.

WINE: In cooking, gives a certain indefinable something unobtainable any other way. The alcohol all evaporates, so teetotallers need not worry. Theoretically, you have white wine in veal, chicken, and fish dishes, and red in beef, mutton, and pork; but in fact (unless the dish is going to *appear* white, when the red wine would make it pink) you can use either in anything. Instead of red wine, you can use beer; instead of white, sherry or dry cider (it must *be* dry – those little bottles of very sweet cider are enough to ruin any dish). Never add wine just before serving: it must cook for a few minutes, to remove any acid taste.

YOGHOURT: Comes in cartons and bottles. Eat it straight, with sugar, or with fruit; or use instead of sour cream in Austro-Hungarian dishes or soups. Don't use flavoured ones in savoury cooking.

## CHAPTER 3

# Breakfast

IN my experience, people who live in bedsitters are not strong on breakfast: a cup of Nescafé, a snatched crust, and they are out of the building on the run. However, perfectly good breakfasts can of course be made on a gas ring, and there are always Sundays; so perhaps this is the place to mention a few absolutely basic things like bacon and eggs.

## Toast

It sounds too simple to mention, but if you are always burning the toast, and getting a sooty taste when you have scraped it, the answer is to *bang* the toast hard; and remember to wipe the cinders off the knife.

## Porridge

In a Scottish household, those who know how to make porridge are occasionally required to get up in the morning and actually do so; consequently when I was in Scotland I took care never to learn. However, my mother assures me it is done like this.

Put one cup porridge oats (the flaky-looking ones that need no soaking) with one teaspoon salt and the same amount of water in a pan. Bubble for 5 mins., adding more water if you like it thin. Eat it with milk or cream. Porridge heats up well the second day.

By all means eat sugar or treacle with it if you like; just don't let the Scotsman across the landing see you doing it.

## Boiled Egg

Four minutes in boiling water gives you the white set, the yolk runny, on a large shop egg. Don't bubble too fiercely, or the egg may crack itself against the pan. Hard-boiled egg takes 7–10 mins.

## Poached Egg

Heat salted water to boiling; break egg on to saucer; lower gas so that the bubbling practically ceases, and slide egg into water; 2–3 mins. is enough.

## Scrambled Egg

Put two eggs, a small lump of butter, salt, pepper, a *little* top of the milk, and onion powder if you have it, into a small pan. Stir constantly over low gas, and stop *just before* it looks done. It always cooks itself a bit more, before you can get it eaten. You can melt the butter first if you like, and beat the egg first, but it isn't really necessary. Alternatively you can make the best scrambled eggs in the world by cooking them over boiling water; but who's going to bother at that time in the morning?

## Eggs and Bacon

Start with the bacon, then the egg can cook in its fat. Only thing to remember is, don't get the fat too hot, or the egg will be all brown and tough beneath before the top is done.

## Kippers

Put on some water to boil. Put the kipper in a jug. Pour boiling water on to it, and do something else while it sits for 10 mins. This is the painless way; but if you have no jug, fry them for about 4 mins. each side, with a lid on if possible. (Frozen kippers must be thawed before cooking in a jug.)

✳✳✳✳✳✳✳✳✳✳✳✳✳✳✳✳✳✳✳✳✳✳✳✳✳

CHAPTER 4

# *Soup*

IT is simply not worth while making your own soup in a bed-sitter. You cannot start monkeying about with a stockpot, and there are dozens and dozens of excellent packet, tinned, condensed, and cube soups on the market for you to choose from. For some reason packets at the moment have a higher reputation than tins: possibly because they were not invented during the war, when tinned soup got its bad name. Actually all kinds can be good or bad: tins are quicker but heavier to carry home; packets are fine but take a little longer; and some have an irritating way of being made up only for a family of six, and priced accordingly. If you have saved any water from cooking vegetables, or have some chicken bones lying about, by all means add this stock to the contents of a packet; but they are fine anyway.

## WAYS OF ADDING TO TINNED AND PACKET SOUPS

*Chopped parsley* on a vegetable soup gives it an undeservedly authentic look. *Toast* cut in little cubes and thrown into soup at very last moment. *Watercress* or *Chives* chopped and sprinkled on a cold soup like tinned Vichyssoise. *Grated Cheese* on an onion soup or a minestrone. *Cream, sour cream,* or *yoghourt* (in small quantities) dumped into the middle of each plate of tomato soup.

## WAYS OF MAKING A SOUP INTO A MEAL FOR YOURSELF

### Sausage Balls

1–2 tablespoons sausage meat      pinch of mixed herbs
1 egg      ½ slice crumbled bread

Mix thoroughly together; form into little balls about the size of a cork and drop into any cooking soup. (They need about 10 mins.)

### Liver Dumplings

2 oz. liver      pinch mixed herbs
1 slice bread      1 small onion
salt, pepper

Chop onion very finely indeed; squeeze bread out in water; chop liver finely. Mix with seasonings, form into little balls, and poach in the soup (i.e. drop them into hot soup and keep it just below boiling point) for 15 mins.

### Potato Dumplings

2 tablespoons left-over      1 dessertspoon flour
  mashed potatoes

Mix thoroughly; form into little balls; poach in cooking soup 10 mins. (You can also buy a potato dumpling mixture in a packet.)

### Ravioli in Soup See page 76.

************************

CHAPTER 5

# Main-Course Dishes for the Evening Meal

## SAUSAGES

SAUSAGES, as we know them, are either pork, beef, or frankfurters. Pork are more expensive than beef; the beef have a more peppery flavour. Small skinless sausages are the cheapest of the pork variety, and are very nice; the kind with skins should be pricked with a fork so that they do not burst. Sausages need little fat, as they exude plenty of their own. Frankfurters can be bought in tins or from delicatessen shops; they are generally already cooked and can be heated in water.

### Sausage and Smash

4 pork or beef sausages          1 tin condensed vegetable soup
a little fat

Fry sausages over medium flame 10 mins.; pour contents of tin into pan, and stir until heated, 3–4 mins. (15 mins.)

### Sausage and Mash (real potato)

4 sausages                    nut of butter
2 or 3 potatoes               spoonful of milk, salt, pepper
fat for frying

First fry sausages 7 mins. Remove pan from ring, and boil potatoes (20 mins.); put back sausages, and while they are finishing (5 mins.), mash the potatoes, add butter and milk. (35 mins.)

## Sausage and Mash (instant potato)

4 sausages                    cupful milk, or milk and water
instant potato
nut of butter

Fry sausages on medium flame 10 mins.; remove. Heat cupful milk or milk and water till it nearly boils; remove, and stir in instant potato until thick enough, while sausages reheat; add butter to potato. (15 mins.)

## Devilled Sausages

4 sausages                    tomato paste
1 tablespoon chutney          fat for frying
1 teaspoon mustard (any kind)

Fry sausages 5 mins. in a little fat. Meanwhile mix chutney, mustard, and a good squeeze of tomato paste. Split sausages lengthwise; spread mixture on them; cook 5 mins. more, chutney side upwards. (12 mins.)

## Sausage and Carrot Ragoût

2–4 sausages                  lemon juice
1 small tin carrots           herbs
1 onion, chopped              fat for frying

Fry onion and sausages together for 10 mins. Add carrots (without their liquid), herbs, a good squeeze of lemon juice. Mix; simmer for a few minutes. (15 mins.)

## Scotch Eggs (to be eaten cold, perhaps with salad; two helpings)

3 eggs                        fat for deep frying
½ lb. sausage meat            breadcrumbs

Hard-boil two eggs. Meanwhile separate white from yolk of third egg. Peel hard-boiled eggs; brush with white of egg;

make a casing of the sausage meat round each; roll in yolk of egg and then breadcrumbs. Fry in deep fat 5 mins. Allow to cool. (25 mins.)

## Sauerkraut and Frankfurters (makes two helpings)

1 tin (or ½ lb.) sauerkraut    1 rasher bacon
1 tin frankfurters

Fry rasher, and meanwhile open tins and drain sauerkraut and frankfurters. Mix, and add to bacon; simmer 15 mins. (20 mins.)

## Spiced Frankfurters

| | |
|---|---|
| 1 small tin frankfurters or cocktail sausages | ½ teaspoon mustard |
| 1 dessertspoon flour | 1 teaspoon vinegar |
| 1 tablespoon tomato paste or 2 tablespoons ketchup | 1 teaspoon sugar |

Mix flour with half a cup of water; put over gentle flame, and slowly add everything else but the frankfurters. Cook gently in saucepan until it thickens; split frankfurters and add to pan. Simmer 5 mins. (15 mins.)

## Danish Bracelets and Chips

| | |
|---|---|
| ¼ lb. sausage meat | 1 tomato |
| 2 rashers | fat for frying |
| 2 or 3 potatoes | salt, water |

Peel potatoes and boil 10 mins. in salted water. Meanwhile form sausage meat into two flat patties, with bacon round the edge pegged in place with headless matchstick. Slice tomato. Remove potatoes from water; dry.

Heat enough fat to cover bottom of pan; fry potatoes at one side of pan, bracelets at the other. When bracelets have done 7 mins. on one side, turn over and lay slice of tomato on each; fry another 7 mins. Fry at medium heat throughout. (25–30 mins.)

## Creole Sausage Casserole

| | |
|---|---|
| 2 sausages | pinch chilli powder |
| 1 onion | salt, pepper, garlic (optional) |
| 1 tomato | meat extract (optional), water |
| ⅓ cup rice | |

Fry sausages on all sides, with chopped onion and chopped clove of garlic. When onion is golden, add a chopped tomato, pinch of chilli powder, salt, pepper, rice, and a cupful of water or water-and-meat-extract. Simmer ½ hr. (40 mins.)

## Swedish Sausage Casserole

| | |
|---|---|
| 2 sausages | flour |
| 1 onion | fat for frying |
| 1 or 2 potatoes, sliced | herbs, bay leaf, salt, pepper |
| 1 or 2 carrots, sliced | meat extract (optional) |

Fry onion gently in fat until golden, remove from gas, stir in flour; gradually add small cupful water or water-and-meat-extract. Put back on medium flame; add potatoes, sausages, carrots, herbs, bay leaf, salt, pepper. Boil very gently for 30 mins. You can fry the sausages with the onions if you prefer them crisp. (40 mins.)

## BACON

Bacon, the great stand-by: bacon and eggs, liver and bacon; bacon and tomatoes – no need to introduce it. No need, either, to buy *back* (with a large piece of lean and a large piece of fat), when *streaky* (mixed stripes of lean and fat) is so good. If you eat it only from time to time, a vacuum pack is a sort of short-term tin: keep the unopened packet till you need it, up to a week or two, without fear of it going bad. A bit of bacon improves almost any casserole; it gives that extra pep to vegetable dishes. (See under VEGETABLES.) Perhaps I had better get on with the recipes before I become too lyrical.

## Danish Bacon and Potatoes

3 cooked potatoes, mashed    2 rashers bacon, chopped
1 or 2 onions    tomatoes

Fry onions 5 mins.; add bacon, fry 5 mins. more. Add mash
and mix thoroughly. If you have a grill, eat with grilled
tomatoes, or fry some with the bacon. (15 mins.; or 35 mins.
if you have to cook the potatoes first.)

## Dixie Casserole

2 or 3 rashers bacon    1 dessertspoon flour
1 small tin sweetcorn    1 cup milk or less
2 eggs (optional)

First hard-boil eggs if you are using them. Then fry bacon
until crisp; pour off fat till about a tablespoon remains. Add
flour, over gentle heat, till fat is absorbed. Add liquid from
tin, gradually, and then milk until you have added one cup in
all. Stir till it thickens; add corn, bacon, and halved hard-
boiled eggs. Simmer 10 mins. (20 mins. without eggs; 30
mins. with eggs.)

## Bacon and Apples

3 or 4 rashers bacon    2 teaspoons sugar
1 large cooking apple

Fry bacon and push to edge of pan; fry sliced apple in the
fat, sprinkling sugar over as it cooks. Eat together. (15 mins.)

## Poor Man's Goulash

2 tomatoes or tomato paste    2 potatoes
1 onion    paprika (essential)
1 or 2 rashers bacon    salt

Start by boiling potatoes for at least 10 mins. Fry onion and
bacon 7 mins. Add a quarter teaspoon paprika, salt, chopped

tomatoes (or good squeeze of paste and a little water). Stir.
Add potatoes, and simmer for as long as it takes them to
cook. If you have some sour milk around, add a tablespoon
at the very end. (30 mins.)

(*Bacon recipes are also to be found under* VEGETABLES, *page*
63, *and* PASTA, *page* 70.)

## LIVER AND KIDNEY

These, being considered offal by some people, are fortunately
cheap; they cook fast and taste good. Two warnings: they go
off quicker than other meat, so eat them the day you buy
them, in warm weather; and they all get like leather if you
cook them too long or too hard. Kidneys have a hard white
core and a skin, which you remove. With liver, the darker
and softer the better; and lambs' or calves' livers are the best.
(Avoid those light-coloured slabs of ox liver with the tubes.)

### Liver and Bacon

| | |
|---|---|
| ¼ lb. liver | 1 tomato (optional) |
| 1 or 2 rashers | 2 teaspoons flour |
| 1 onion | |

Begin gently frying rashers, and when they have given off
some fat, add slices of liver which you have dipped in flour,
and onion chopped very fine; fry quickly on each side; then
lower gas and cook very slowly for about 7 mins. each side
or more, depending on the thickness of the slices. Add
tomato 5 mins. before the end, if you want to. Pour the
gravy over the liver and bacon when you lift it on to plate.
You can also fry potatoes beforehand, but use only bacon
fat, for the sake of the taste. (20 mins.)

### Liver Josephine

| | |
|---|---|
| 1 onion | 3 tablespoons water |
| ¼ lb. liver | salt, pepper |
| 1 dessertspoon tomato paste | fat for frying |

Fry onion for 5 mins., meanwhile cut liver into little cubes and sprinkle them with flour. Add to onion; add salt, pepper, tomato paste, and water. Stir; simmer gently 10 mins. (20 mins.)

## Venetian Liver

¼ lb. lamb's liver (if possible)  olive oil
4 or 5 onions                     salt, pepper

Cut up onion finely, and put in saucepan with about a tablespoon of olive oil and stew very gently for 20 mins. with lid on. Cut liver into paper-thin slices; add to onion with salt and pepper; simmer 5 mins. more (or longer, if the liver wasn't lambs' liver after all). (30 mins.)

## Fried Kidneys (fried, yes – but *gently*)

2 kidneys    2 cooked potatoes
1 onion      herbs; pepper

Chop up onions and kidneys; slice potatoes. Fry onion hard for 7 mins. Add kidneys and potatoes, sprinkle with herbs and pepper, and fry for 5–7 mins. more; gentle heat. (15–20 mins.)

## Turbigo Kidneys

1 kidney                        2 oz. mushrooms
2 sausages (preferably          1 teaspoon tomato paste
  chipolatas)                   1 dessertspoon flour
1 onion                         2 bay leaves

Halve kidneys when removing core. Fry kidney and sausages for a minute or two, so that all sides are browned. Remove. Put in chopped onion and chopped mushroom, and fry 5 mins. Add flour, tomato paste, bay leaves, and 3 tablespoons water. Stir. Put back kidney and sausage, and simmer very gently ¼ hour. (35 mins.)

## Kidneys and Corn

2 kidneys    1 small tin sweetcorn

Divide kidneys into four pieces; fry gently 10 mins. Heat sweetcorn; pour off some of the liquid; re-heat kidneys by sitting them on sweetcorn over almost extinct flame. (15 mins.)

## Chicken Livers and Egg with Chips

4 chicken livers or more    2 potatoes
2 eggs

Slice potatoes; beat eggs in cup; pick over chicken livers and chop. Fry potatoes 15 mins. Push to side of pan, or remove and drain. Put livers on one side of the remaining space in pan, eggs on the other. They will take about the same length of time to cook – not long. (20 mins.)

## Chicken Livers on Toast

¼ lb. chicken livers    olive oil or butter
2 oz. mushrooms    lemon juice (optional)
bread

Fry mushrooms gently in a little oil or butter 5 mins. Add chicken livers, chopped, and stir about for a minute or two till cooked. Squeeze over lemon juice. Drain for a minute if possible; lay on toast. (10 mins.)
(See also CHICKEN LIVER RISOTTO, page 73)

## Tripe Catalan

I am no fonder of boiled knitting than anyone else, but I assure you that this is rather different from normal tripe. It really is edible.

½ lb. tripe    handfuls of herbs
2 onions    2 tomatoes
salt, pepper    1 dessertspoon tomato paste

Prepare a pot of water with the seasonings and one of the onions in it; into this, averting your eyes, empty the piece of damp blanket you will have received from the butcher. Clap the lid on and boil gently for 2 hrs.

Then take it out, cut in strips, flour them; fry them with other ingredients and more herbs till onions are soft. (2¼ hrs.)

## EGGS

### Omelette

An omelette is the quickest form of cooked food there is, capable of many variations. A plain omelette is made like this.

2 eggs            salt, pepper
butter or oil (*a very little*)

Beat up eggs in basin, with salt and pepper. Heat a very little fat in a clean frying pan; and when it is very hot – smoking and almost about to go up in flames – pour in eggs. Wait just long enough for egg to drain completely from the bowl, then pull back mixture from sides of pan with a spoon. Just *before* the egg is set, when it is still 'dribbly', fold it over and slide it out of the pan. Cooking time 45 seconds. (*Don't* use milk. *Don't* use too much fat – it will become greasy. *Don't* cook too long – speed is vital.)

*Cheese omelette*. Sprinkle a dessertspoonful of grated cheese on to the omelette just before you fold it over.

*Bacon omelette*. Fry a chopped-up rasher of bacon before you start the omelette; remove the bits and any surplus of fat from the pan, make the omelette, and add the bits just before you fold the omelette over.

*Herb omelette*. Mix a handful of herbs – at least some of them fresh – into the eggs before you start.

*Tomato omelette*. Fry slices of tomato, and remove from pan; add to omelette before you fold it over.

COOKING TO STAY ALIVE

## Spanish Omelette

| 1 cooked potato | 1 rasher bacon |
| 1 onion | 2 eggs |
| 1 tomato | salt, pepper; fat for frying |

You can use any other oddments instead of the onion, potato, tomato, and bacon. Chop it all up small, and fry in as little fat as possible. Beat eggs with salt and pepper in bowl, and pour into hot frying pan; but do not try to fold it over – it will be too thick. Leave until just set – no longer. (10 mins.)

## Potato Omelette

| 2 cooked potatoes | salt, pepper |
| 2 eggs | fat for frying |

Make it just like a Spanish omelette, frying potatoes first. (5 mins.)

## Piperade

| 2 or more eggs | 2 tomatoes (optional) |
| 2 green pimentoes | salt, pepper |
| 1 onion (optional) | oil for frying |

Cut up pimento and remove seeds and white membrane. Chop onions. Fry both till soft (10 mins.); add tomatoes, salt, pepper. Break eggs into cup, and tip the lot into the pan, stirring them to break them and mix them in. This dish tastes extremely good with just the eggs and pimentoes. (15 mins.)

## Scrambled Eggs and Potatoes (if you have a bowl that will sit on your saucepan)

| 2 or 3 potatoes | 1 teaspoon butter |
| 2 eggs | salt, pepper |
| 1 dessertspoon top of milk | |

Put the potatoes on to boil in salted water. After five minutes'
boiling, put the eggs, butter, salt, and pepper in bowl sitting
on the top of the pan; beat lightly with a fork, and then stir
frequently to keep the setting egg from sticking to bowl.
Remove bowl just *before* eggs are quite set. Actually makes
better scrambled eggs than in a pan. Can be done over any
cooking vegetable. (20 mins.)

## Scrambled Eggs and Mushrooms

| | |
|---|---|
| 3 eggs | butter |
| ¼ lb. mushrooms | salt, pepper; top of the milk |

Wash mushrooms, but you need not peel them; chop up
stalks finely, and fry the lot gently in butter for about six
minutes. Beat two eggs lightly in cup with a little salt,
pepper, and top of the milk. Add to mushrooms, stir round
till set. Eat with toast. (12 mins.)

## Oeufs Mollets Fines Herbes (This classy title conceals a
very simple and delightful dish to be made after a week-
end in the country.)

| | |
|---|---|
| 2 or 3 eggs | a handful of chopped *fresh* herbs |
| butter (essential) | (especially parsley) |

Boil eggs in water for 4 mins. Remove; run under cold tap if
possible, and shell, but keep whole. Turn them gently in
butter that is hot but not brown; sprinkle herbs over them in
the pan; remove with all the butter and eat. (12 mins.)

## Eggs in Cheese

| | |
|---|---|
| 2 or 3 eggs | 1 dessertspoon grated cheese |
| 1 teaspoon butter, 1 dessert-spoon flour, 1 cup milk for white sauce | salt, pepper |

Boil eggs 4 mins.; remove, peel, and halve. Make white
sauce by melting butter, mixing in flour, gradually add milk.

When it thickens, add cheese; simmer 7 mins. Add eggs to re-heat. Sprinkle grated cheese on plate. (20 mins.)

## Italian Sandwich

| | |
|---|---|
| 1 slice ham | 1 egg |
| 1 slice of cheese (Gruyère for choice) | butter |

Melt a little butter in frying pan. Put the slice of ham in, with the cheese on it, topped by the egg. The egg white will overflow, and must be scooped back to begin with. Put a plate over it, and cook gently about 4 mins. – until the egg is set. (7 mins.)

## Egg Casserole (more elaborate, this, but it makes a fine full meal)

| | |
|---|---|
| 2 eggs | $\frac{1}{4}$ teaspoon French |
| 1 tin condensed tomato soup | mustard |
| 1 onion (optional) | salt, pepper |
| 1 heaped dessertspoon grated | 2 small slices bread |
| cheese (mousetrap will do | oil or butter |
| fine) | 3 tablespoons milk |

Fry chopped onion and bread till onion is golden and bread crisp. Add cheese, soup, mustard, salt, and pepper over low gas; stir gently until it is one gooey mass. Add eggs and milk beaten lightly together; stir once; let it cook gently until the egg part seems set – about 5 mins. (20 mins.)

## Shropshire Eggs

| | |
|---|---|
| 2 tablespoons mashed potatoes | fat for deep frying |
| (left-over or instant) | $\frac{1}{2}$ teaspoon curry powder |
| 2 eggs, hard-boiled | 1 tin cooked tomatoes or |
| 1 egg, raw | spinach purée |
| breadcrumbs | |

Mix curry powder with mashed potatoes; shape around eggs, to form larger egg; roll in lightly beaten raw egg, then in breadcrumbs. Fry 4 mins. in deep hot fat. Put on clean newspaper to drain, while you quickly heat up the tinned tomatoes or spinach purée. (20 mins. or less if you already have breadcrumbs.)

## VEGETABLES

If meat costs 35p a pound, we think it cheap; if vegetables cost 35p a pound we think them dear. Moral: eat vegetables. Most of these dishes are a meal in themselves, or at least a course in themselves. For some reason people are quite willing to believe that a *familiar* vegetable dish (like Cauliflower Cheese) is nourishing, but have the gravest doubts about unfamiliar ones. So let me assure you that these *are*: and you will notice how often there is a bit of cheese or bacon or egg or sausage meat in them to make up the required balance.

### Cauliflower Cheese

½ small cauliflower
1 teaspoon butter
1 dessertspoon flour
rather less than 1 cup milk

1 tablespoon grated or finely
   chopped cheese
salt, pepper

Put on a pan one-third full of salted water; when it boils, add cauliflower washed and cut in pieces, and a piece of bread to absorb smell; put on lid. Boil 10 mins. (15 if you have included the tough stalks.) Remove lid outside room. Drain.* Make white sauce in small pan by melting butter, stirring in flour, gradually adding milk; when it thickens, add most of the cheese. Cook gently for 5 mins. Add cauliflower; cook 4 mins. more. Sprinkle with remainder of cheese after it is on the plate. (25–30 mins.)

### Cauliflower with Bacon and Onion

½ small cauliflower
1 or 2 rashers bacon
1 onion

1 teaspoon butter, 1 dessertspoon
   flour, small cup milk

63

Exactly like cauliflower cheese until *; then fry onion and rasher in butter in small pan for 10 mins. Add flour (*off* the heat), gradually stir in milk, heat till it thickens, add cauliflower, cook gently 10 mins. (35–40 mins.)

## Stuffed Tomatoes

| | |
|---|---|
| 2 large tomatoes | 1 onion |
| 2 dessertspoons sausage meat (about 2 oz.) | oil for frying, herbs, salt |
| | cooked rice (optional) |

Fry onion for 5 mins. Meanwhile cut off tops of tomatoes and scoop out pulp. Add sausage meat and rice to onions, brown for a minute or two only; remove and add all this to the tomato pulp, with herbs and salt, but NO PEPPER. Stuff the tomatoes with mixture; return to pan and cook 10–15 mins. in oil on medium flame. (25–30 mins.)

## Stuffed Pimentoes

After years of failure on this I have decided that the only way is to stuff the pimentoes with something that needs little cooking, and half-cook the pimentoes first. The alternative seems to be either leathery pimentoes and sloppy stuffing, or firm stuffing with disintegrating pimentoes.

| | |
|---|---|
| 2 green, or red, pimentoes | 1 onion and 1 tomato *or* |
| 2 heaped dessertspoons sausage meat (about 3 oz.) | some left-over gravy or sauce |

Boil some water in saucepan; add cleaned and emptied pimentoes and boil 5 mins. Let stand in water while you fry the chopped onion in oil for 5 mins., add tomato and sausage meat; herbs, salt and any oddments you may have around – e.g., cooked rice, raisins, left-over veg, etc. Throw away water, stuff the softened pimentoes with the mixture from the frying pan, cook gently in a little oil in covered pan for 15 mins., or until the pimentoes look as if they are about to collapse. Eat them before they do. (35 mins.)

## Stuffed Cabbage Leaves

½ cabbage; sausage, onion, tomato, etc., as above

Proceed exactly as for Pimentoes, but roll stuffing in softened cabbage leaves, and pack closely in pan so that they do not collapse. You may need to use 2 or 3 leaves to one roll – it depends how good you are at parcels. (Use inside of cabbage for salad, see p. 105.) (35 mins.)

## Cabbage, Leeks, and Bacon

| | |
|---|---|
| ½ cabbage (or less) | 1 teaspoon butter |
| 2 leeks | 1 dessertspoon flour |
| 1 or 2 rashers bacon | 1 teaspoon meat extract |

Boil cabbage, leeks, and bacon gently for 15 mins. in a cup or so of salted water. Remove. Melt butter in small pan, stir in flour, gradually add liquid from other pan and meat extract. Put back solids to re-heat. (30 mins.)

## Leeks Lucullus

| | |
|---|---|
| 3 leeks (about 1 lb.) | butter |
| 2 or 3 potatoes | top of the milk |
| 1 tablespoon grated cheese | salt, pepper |

Boil leeks and potatoes together in salted water with lid on pan till tender – 15–20 mins. Pour off liquid. Mash leeks and potatoes with a fork; stir in as much butter as you can spare (at least a teaspoon), cheese, creamy milk. Eat with a piece of toast. If you have a grill, sprinkle more cheese and brown the top. This looks like pale green mashed potatoes, but tastes delicious. (25 mins.)

## Ratatouille (two helpings)

This is the most delicious Provençal vegetable stew, to which you can make various additions. Cook it in the autumn, when the right vegetables are cheap. It heats up well.

| | |
|---|---|
| 1 onion | 2 baby marrows (optional) |
| 1 pimento | 2 tablespoons olive oil or more |
| 1 aubergine | garlic |
| 2 tomatoes | |

Chop onion and garlic roughly, and begin to fry very gently in saucepan with lid on. After 10 mins. add chopped pimento and aubergine and marrows. After ten more minutes add tomatoes, preferably peeled. Simmer gently for at least 30 mins. more – preferably 40 – with lid on throughout. Vegetables should all be disintegrating blissfully together at the end. (50 mins.–1 hr.)

*Variation 1 : with scrambled egg*

Cook 2 or more eggs, with butter, pepper, and salt, in bowl on top of ratatouille for last 10 mins., stirring frequently.

*Variation 2 : with egg mixed in*

Stir in 2 eggs 4 mins. before the end.

*Variation 3 : with beef*

Stir in ¼ lb. minced beef 5 mins. before the end – and lie down for an hour after the meal. You'll need to.


## Spanish Peas

| | |
|---|---|
| 1 tin peas (not processed) *or* | 1 dessertspoon flour |
| 1 lb. fresh peas | 1 nut of butter |
| 2 sausages | tomato paste, herbs, |
| 1 rasher bacon | pepper |

Fry sausages and rasher in saucepan in as little fat as possible for 10 mins. Remove from pan. Add flour to fat in pan; mix; gradually add liquid from the peas – about 1 cup. Stir till it thickens. Add everything else and put back bacon and sausages. Simmer 7–10 mins. (25 mins. with tinned peas.)

With fresh peas, cook them before you begin all this, and add another 15 mins. to the time.

## Belgian Sprouts

1 small packet frozen sprouts
  or ½ lb. fresh sprouts
1 small can celery *or* 1 head
  celery chopped and washed

1 dessertspoon (or more)
  grated cheese
1 dessertspoon flour
1 teaspoon butter *or* 1
  tablespoon oil; salt,
  pepper

Begin by cooking the sprouts and celery. If you are using fresh vegetables, put them in boiling salted water and boil for 15 mins. If you use frozen sprouts, follow instructions on the packet. Keep the liquid the vegetables have cooked in, and make a sauce from it by melting the butter, mixing in flour, adding liquid gradually. Add cheese, simmer 5 mins. Put back sprouts and celery; simmer 5 mins. more. (35–40 mins.)

## Swedes and Bacon

1 large or 2 small swedes
3 rashers bacon

1 onion (optional)

Slice swedes; cut rashers in two and remove rinds. Layer three bits bacon, half the swedes, the other three bits bacon, the rest of the swedes, in pan or earthenware casserole on asbestos. Add two cups water (more later, if it seems to be drying up) and simmer till swedes are tender – 1 hr. If you add onion, put it with bacon. (1 hr or more.)

## Broccoli Cheese

1 packet frozen broccoli
2 dessertspoons cheese

1 egg
butter

Cook broccoli in boiling salted water according to directions on packet. Mix egg, cheese, and a nut of butter (about 1 teaspoon) *either* in bowl that will cook on top of boiling-broccoli pan, *or* in pan to cook when broccoli is done. Either way, stir egg and cheese mixture over very gentle heat till egg sets; mix with broccoli. (15–20 mins.)

## Broad Beans and Bacon

| | |
|---|---|
| 1 small tin broad beans | parsley |
| 2 rashers bacon | 1 teaspoon vinegar |
| 1 dessertspoon flour | pepper |

Fry bacon without extra fat, remove, and stir flour into fat in pan. Gradually add liquid from tin of beans; stir till it thickens; if too thick, add extra milk and/or water. Add beans and flavouring and vinegar. Simmer 5 mins. Add bacon; stir; simmer 5 mins. more. (No salt mentioned, because bacon should be salt enough.) (20 mins.)

## Toucan Mush

Your two cans contain (1) peeled tomatoes, (2) broad beans. And you need also:

| | |
|---|---|
| 1 onion | fat for frying |
| 1 tablespoon grated cheese | |

Fry the onion till golden and soft; add the two cans *without* their liquid; cook 10 mins.; sprinkle grated cheese, cook 3 mins. more until cheese begins to melt. (20 mins.)

## Potato Ragoût

| | |
|---|---|
| 2 or 3 potatoes | herbs, parsley, bay leaf; salt |
| 2 or 3 onions | and pepper |
| 1 dessertspoon flour | ½ pint water |
| 1 teaspoon meat extract | butter or oil |

Heat a nut of butter (or dessertspoon of oil) in saucepan; stir in flour; gradually add water and meat extract. Put in everything else, and cook gently for ½ hr. The lower the gas, the longer the cooking, the nicer this one is. (40 mins.)

## La Truffado

| | |
|---|---|
| 2 or 3 potatoes (or more) | 2 dessertspoons bits of cheese |
| 1 rasher bacon (optional) | (not grated, not processed) |
| oil or butter | |

Slice potatoes very thinly, and fry gently 15 mins. in oil or butter. Add little bits of cheese and allow them to melt. (Processed cheese doesn't melt properly.) Scoop it all out on to a plate – all stuck together, as it will be – and eat. (20 mins.)

## Lentils

School lentils have put most of us off them for life; but unless you really detest the flavour, give them another try. They are cheap and comforting in cold weather, and there is no need to soak them or boil them for hours before they become eatable (though those with difficult digestions may prefer all dried pulses to be pre-soaked). The large brown lentils require longer treatment than the small red.

## Lentils as a Vegetable See page 37.

## Bacon and Lentils (two helpings)

| | |
|---|---|
| 2 rashers *or* a small lump of | garlic, pepper, herbs |
| bacon or gammon | 1 pint water |
| ½ cup lentils | |

Fry bacon slightly for a few minutes, or brown lump on all sides. Add water, lentils, garlic, pepper, herbs (optional), and boil. With rashers it will take 25 mins. With a lump, it will depend on its size and it is better to cook it more gently for an hour or more. (30 mins.–1¼ hrs.)

## Egg Lentillade (two helpings)

| | |
|---|---|
| ½ cup lentils | oil |
| 1 onion | garlic (optional) |
| 2 eggs | mint (optional) |

Fry the chopped onion, garlic, and lentils in oil for a few minutes; add a pint of water and a sprig of mint and boil for 30 mins. Let it get cool; meanwhile hard-boil two or more eggs, chop them in quarters, and add to the cold lentils. If they seem a bit dry, add more oil to the cold lentils. This mixture is a good stuffing for tomatoes if you have any of it left over. (35 mins. cooking time; about 50 mins. all told.)

## Corn on the Cob

2 frozen or fresh corn cobs      salt
butter (essential)

Cook cobs in boiling salted water 15 mins. Drain. Spread butter over the cobs, and eat in your fingers, tearing off the kernels with your teeth. Paper napkins are a help for those who find they get the butter in their ears. (20 mins.)

## Carrot Ragoût

| | |
|---|---|
| 2 carrots | 1 rasher of bacon |
| 1 potato | herbs, salt, pepper |
| 1 small onion | 1 teaspoon fat |

Peel and slice carrots, potato, and onion. Fry onion gently in saucepan for a few minutes, add potato, carrots, and chopped rasher, and turn in fat for a minute or two. Add small cup water, herbs, salt, pepper. Simmer gently 40 mins. Keep an eye on it to see it does not burn. (1 hr.)

# PASTA

## Spaghetti

There are innumerable different sauces for spaghetti; or if you are feeling really poor and hungry you can simply eat it with butter and grated cheese, or even just with butter. A few possibilities are given below; but the great thing is to experiment for yourself. However you cook the sauce, you cook the spaghetti itself like this:

25 long strands of spaghetti     a panful of boiling water
   (at least)                           salt

Into a panful of boiling salted water lower your spaghetti by holding the ends in one hand while the other ends soften in the water. You will gradually be able to wind the whole lot into the pan. Boil until it is just tender – 10–15 mins. Don't go on till it is all soggy.

Other forms of Italian pasta are cooked in exactly the same way, but take a longer or shorter time depending on what they are made with. They should all have some 'bite' left when you take them out of the water.

## Standard Sauce

1 onion                salt, pepper
1 rasher of bacon     garlic (optional)
2 or 3 tomatoes       tomato paste (optional)
                               grated Parmesan cheese

First cook the spaghetti and drain it. Then fry onion and bacon until bacon is crisp and onion soft – just under 10 mins. Add tomatoes, the flavourings, and a little of the cheese. Add the spaghetti to heat up; move out on to plate and sprinkle with more cheese. ($\frac{1}{2}$ hr including spaghetti cooking.)

## Spaghetti Bolognese

1 onion                $\frac{1}{4}$ teaspoon French mustard
$\frac{1}{4}$ lb. minced beef     grated Parmesan cheese
tomato paste         oil for frying
salt, pepper, herbs

Cook spaghetti. Drain. Fry the onion, and when it is soft add a squeeze of tomato paste, the seasonings, and a tablespoon of water. Stir. Put in mince, and break it up with a spoon, stirring until it is brown, not pink. If it seems stiff or dry, put in a little water. Add spaghetti to re-heat; sprinkle with cheese just before you eat it. Very filling. ($\frac{1}{2}$ hr including spaghetti.)

COOKING TO STAY ALIVE

## Fish Spaghetti

1 small tin anchovies
  or sardines
1 onion

1 tomato or squeeze of tomato
  paste
nuts (optional)

Cook spaghetti. Drain. Fry onion in the oil from the fish tin;
add tomato and nuts. Stir. Add spaghetti to re-heat. (25
mins. including spaghetti.)

## Mushroom Spaghetti

1 or 2 rashers bacon,
  chopped
grated cheese

¼ lb. mushrooms, washed but not
  peeled
oil or butter for frying

Cook spaghetti. Drain. Fry the mushrooms with the bacon
gently in butter or oil for 6 mins. or so. When they are soft,
add a good sprinkling of cheese and the spaghetti to re-heat.
(25 mins. including spaghetti.)

## Chicken Liver Spaghetti

¼ lb. chicken livers or less
1 or 2 mushrooms or more
  (washed)

1 onion
parsley, herbs; salt, pepper
oil or butter for frying

Fry onion 5 mins.; lower heat, add washed chicken livers
and chopped mushrooms; fry gently another 5 mins. or so.
Add seasonings, and spaghetti to re-heat. (30 mins. including spaghetti.)

## Balkan Spaghetti

2 dessertspoons yoghourt
2 cloves garlic
tomato paste

pepper
oil (or better still butter)

First cook spaghetti. Drain. Chop garlic and fry for 5 mins.
in butter or oil with a dessertspoon tomato paste and a

sprinkle of pepper. Put in spaghetti to re-heat, add yoghourt, give it a good stir, and take it out of the pan. For this one you may chop up the spaghetti, without losing face. (20 mins.)

## Risotto

One way of making risotto is simply to cook some rice (as on page 78) and eat it with the same kind of sauces as spaghetti. On the other hand, the normal Italian method of doing a risotto is particularly well adapted to a gas ring. Here's how.

## Mushroom Risotto

| | |
|---|---|
| 1 onion (chopped) | ½ cup rice |
| 2–4 oz. mushrooms (washed, chopped, but not peeled) | soup cube<br>grated Parmesan cheese |

First heat some water in a kettle and stand near fire. Then fry the onion and mushrooms in butter for 5 mins. in a saucepan. Add rice, and cook another 2 or 3 mins. on medium flame. Now pour hot water over soup cube, and add this 'stock' to the pan – it will bubble alarmingly, but never mind. Stir it over medium flame 20 mins., adding more water and/or 'stock' if it looks like drying up. (But there should be no extra liquid at the end.) Wine or saffron sound exotic, but if you can manage them they improve the dish. (30 mins.)

## Chicken Liver Risotto

| | |
|---|---|
| 1 onion | 1 or 2 cubes chicken soup |
| 2–4 oz. chicken livers | ½ cup rice |
| mushrooms (optional) | salt, pepper |

First heat water in kettle and mix soup cubes with one cup hot water. Fry onion 5 mins. Add washed chicken livers, fry gently 3 mins. *and remove livers from pan.* Add mushrooms and ½ cup rice; stir in fat 3 mins. or so. Now add the soup stock, and ½ cup hot water, and boil with lid off for 20 mins. Stir often, add more water if necessary (but there should be no extra liquid at the end). When rice looks done, put back chicken livers to reheat (if you leave them in the whole time, you might as well heel your shoes with them). (35 mins.)

## Quickie Risotto

½ cup rice          1 large packet onion, beef, or minestrone
3 cups water        soup

Mix soup packet with a little water. Put in pan with rice and the rest of the water: boil 15 mins., adding more water if it looks like drying up. You can add one or two halved hard-boiled eggs at the end to make it more substantial. (20 mins.)

## Fish Risotto (another rather un-Italian activity)

1 small packet frozen cod,    1 tin condensed mushroom
  haddock, etc.          soup
½ cup rice          1½ cups water

Cook fish and rice together with water for 15 mins. Stir in condensed soup; leave 2 mins. to heat; eat. (20 mins.)

## Macaroni

You can cook macaroni with all the sauces listed with spaghetti; and if you make heavy weather of heaving yards and yards of spaghetti in and out of the pan, macaroni is perhaps a better idea for you.

Alternatively, here is the recipe for the good old English dish of

## Macaroni Cheese

½ cup macaroni         1 teaspoon butter, 1
2 heaped dessertspoons grated    dessertspoon flour, 1
  cheese            cup milk for white
                 sauce

Boil macaroni in salted water until just soft – about 15 mins. Drain. Make white sauce (as on page 42), melting butter, mixing in flour, gradually adding milk. Add cheese and macaroni, and simmer 5 mins. Sprinkle with more cheese before eating. If by any chance you have a grill, brown the top under it. (30 mins.)

## Mushroom Macaroni

½ cup macaroni     1 tin condensed mushroom soup
salt

Boil macaroni in salted water until just soft – about 15 mins. Drain off water. Empty soup over macaroni, stir over low flame for a minute or two. Don't heat fiercely, or soup gets too liquid. (20 mins.)

## Carbonara Macaroni

2 or 3 rashers bacon or 2 slices ham     ½ cup macaroni
1 egg     grated cheese

Cook macaroni in boiling salted water 15 mins. Drain. In frying pan, fry bacon or ham cut into strips. When crisp, add beaten egg and stir till it is almost set. Quickly add macaroni, stir once, scoop it out of pan, and sprinkle with grated cheese. (25 mins.)

## Curried Macaroni

2 onions     1 tablespoon sugar
1 apple     1 teaspoon curry powder
½ cup macaroni     oil or fat for frying
1 dessertspoon vinegar

Fry chopped apple and onions for 5 mins. Add sugar and curry powder mixed into vinegar; stir over *gentle* flame. Add 1 pint water; bring just to boiling point, add macaroni, and simmer ½ hour. (40 mins.)

(See also CURRY SALAD, page 108, for leftover macaroni.)

## Gnocchi (this is so quick that it is worth mastering)

| | |
|---|---|
| 1 small carton cream cheese | 1 tablespoon grated Parme- |
| 2 tablespoons flour | san (plus some for sprink- |
| 1 beaten egg | ling) |

Mix all this together, form into little balls (each about one half teaspoonful of mixture), and roll in a little more flour. Meanwhile have a pan of salted water on the boil, and drop the little nuts of gnocchi into it. In theory, they are done when they float, but if they float right away, then cook for about 4 mins. Drain, and sprinkle with Parmesan cheese. (10 mins.)

## Ravioli

No one in a bedsitter is going to embark on making their own ravioli, pounding the herbs into the meat, rolling the pasta, and singing Neapolitan songs in a throaty tenor. But if you happen to live near a good Italian shop, buy half a pound of fresh-made ravioli (i.e. don't buy it if it looks glazed, dried-up, and old) and cook it in one of these ways:

## Buttered Ravioli

| | | |
|---|---|---|
| ¼ lb. ravioli | salt | butter |

Drop the ravioli into boiling, slightly salted, water; cook till no white line of uncooked flour shows when you break one in half – 10–25 mins. depending on the thickness of the pasta; pick them out of water, put a lump of butter on them, and eat.

NB – Don't go on and on cooking fresh ravioli in the hope that it will become as soft as the tinned sort. It shouldn't. (10–25 mins.)

## Ravioli in Soup

| | |
|---|---|
| 1 tin clear consommé or 2 beef bouillon cubes | ¼ lb ravioli |

Make exactly as above, but drop the ravioli into simmering consommé or bouillon instead of water; and eat or drink (what *do* you do to soup?) the consommé with the ravioli.

## Ravioli in Tomato Sauce

Purists are against this, as you are supposed to be able to taste the stuffing of the ravioli, and you won't if it is wrapped in sauce. However, if you have good reason to prefer *not* to taste the stuffing, or if you are accustomed to eat it in a sauce . . .

| | |
|---|---|
| 1 onion | salt, pepper |
| 4 tomatoes or 1 small tin tomatoes | garlic |

First boil ravioli; drain. Then fry onion and crushed garlic in butter or oil 5 mins. Add peeled or tinned tomatoes, and simmer to a mush – about 10 mins. If it looks like getting dry, add a little water (not necessary with tinned tomatoes). Add ravioli to re-heat. (40 mins.)


## Frying Pan Pizza (Don't do this if you have a buckled frying pan. Otherwise it is not nearly as tricky as it sounds.)

| | |
|---|---|
| 1 small tin anchovies | olive oil for frying |
| 2 tomatoes, sliced | black olives (optional) |
| 1 breakfast cup flour | cheese, sliced or grated |
| 1 teaspoon baking powder | salt |

Mix flour, baking powder, pinch salt, and 3 tablespoons water. Knead it into a dough – you can be as rough as you like – and manhandle it for several minutes. Roll it out (with a milk bottle) into a round about the size of a tea plate. Heat oil in frying pan to about $\frac{1}{4}$ in. depth. It must be hot but not smoking. EVERYING DEPENDS ON THE HEAT OF THE OIL. Lay pizza carefully in pan (don't let oil spill over on to it or it will come up in a great bubble) and cook 5 mins.; it should be golden brown underneath. Turn over; and lay strips of anchovies, sliced tomatoes, and pieces of cheese on the cooked side. Cook 5 mins. more from moment of turning. (15–20 mins.)

## Pissaladina

| | |
|---|---|
| 1 breakfast cup flour | 4 black olives |
| 1 teaspoon baking powder | 4 onions, chopped |
| salt | |

Simmer onions in a little oil in a saucepan until they are a mush – about 20 mins. Meanwhile make and fry dough exactly as in pizza recipe. Spread the onion mush and stoned halved black olives on the dough when you turn it over. (35 mins.)

## RICE

There are two good ways for you to cook rice on your gas ring, and which you choose depends on whether you care most about speed or about avoiding the need for draining the stuff at the last moment.

Whether you keep the grains apart by keeping them moving, or by coating them with fat, you do *not* need to go through the palaver of rinsing them under the tap, either before or after.

Or you can always buy instant rice, which, though not instant, does finish itself off away from the heat.

*Method 1* is easiest. Put on a large panful of water to boil, with about half a teaspoon salt in it. When it is boiling, throw in rice (about one-third cup for one person, one meal) and go on boiling *hard* for about 12–14 mins. The water must bubble hard so that the grains of rice whirl about and never get a chance to stick together. Test grains of rice by pinching them between finger and thumb; if you feel no hard grit in the centre the rice is done. Don't go on too long. When it is done, pour off the water. No need to rinse. (15–20 mins.)

*Method 2* has the advantage of leaving the gas ring free

during the last 10 minutes of cooking. First put on a kettle to boil. As soon as it boils, heat about a tablespoon of fat in a saucepan, and turn the rice about in it till it is transparent. Then add one and a half times as much water as you have rice – i.e. for $\frac{1}{2}$ cup of rice, you add $\frac{3}{4}$ cup water. Keep it cooking busily, with the lid off, until all the water is just about gone. Then put the lid on, and stand it by the fire while you cook whatever is to go with it – at least 10 mins. (25 mins.)

If you are cooking rice on its own, for a future dish, use the foolproof method described on page 133.

## BEEF

Most cookery books begin with the portrait, in profile, of the Planned Cow. This amiable beast is covered with dotted lines, like a map; and the idea is to show the uninitiated where their piece of beef should come from.

I am sorry to deny my readers this pretty sight. But the trouble with the Planned Cow is that it looks so totally unlike the nameless red hunks that actually appear on the butcher's slab. It is really more use to know what it looks like when you buy it than to know what it looked like when it was somebody's mother (or son).

Ask the names of things you like the look of, and remember next time. In the meantime, content yourself with three simple categories. There is *frying steak*, which should be a rich deep red and rather expensive. The butcher will tell you that it is lovely tender meat and that he is having some for his own dinner: lies, all lies. *Braising steak* is getting on for tough, and *stewing steak* is frankly awful. If you are not squeamish and have a sharp knife and the time to cut off the fouler parts, you can make a very good thing of stewing beef; but it takes time. It often pays to get a slice cut off a roasting joint, if your butcher will let you: you waste so much less of the meat in cutting it up that it can come just as cheap as a vast heap of inexpensive tubes and gristle.

COOKING TO STAY ALIVE

Granted that the beef that you can afford is usually tough, there are three things you can do to make it more tender.

(1) Hit it. Break down the fibres by beating it with the edge of a saucer or the heel of a milk bottle or your wooden spoon. This is noisy but effective; and all but the most superlative steak is improved by it.

(2) Soak it in, or cook it with, something acid – wine, vinegar, lemon juice, tomato, or tomato paste. The acid breaks down the fibres which make it tough.

(3) Cook it *slowly*. Really slow cooking will tenderize anything, even birchbark, in time.

## Steak

I am putting steak into this section because I think it is too risky to serve it to visitors: I hate to think of the number of times I have chawed my way through a tough steak while my hostess wrung her hands and said, 'Oh, dear, the butcher *said* it was tender.' The sad fact is that there is only so much good steak on each animal, and the regular housewife, the restaurateur, and the butcher's friends and relations are all ahead of you in the queue.

However, if you want to experiment on your own, that is a different matter. Here are the basic ways of dealing with it.

## Frying

Rub steak with garlic if you like it, but NO SALT. Cut the fat in two or three places, to stop it curling up. Have fat medium hot in pan; fry quickly 1 min. each side to seal in the juices (and don't prod with a fork or they will all escape again). Turn down gas and fry gently for 5 mins. each side or longer. (NOTE: underdone steak has a better chance of staying tender than steak cooked a solid brown all through.)

## Pan Broiling

Really a method of grilling meat in a frying pan. First prepare steak as for frying; clean frying pan and put on to heat.

After a few minutes, wipe the frying pan over with a greased paper, and hurl your steak on to this almost red-hot surface. Two or three minutes each side should be enough; and at the end it should be dark on the outside and pink within. (If you do potatoes with this, do them in a saucepan beforehand, to leave the frying pan free for the steak alone.)

## Flash-fry Steaks

are medium quality steaks already beaten to a pulp by the butcher. One min. each side in hot fat – NOT MORE.

## Braising

This just means cooking very slowly in a little fat and/or water with the lid on. Use one of the following recipes.

## Neapolitan Steak

¼ lb. braising or frying steak     2 or 3 tomatoes *or* 1 small
oil, garlic, salt, pepper     tin tomatoes

Heat a little oil in saucepan and fry tomatoes very gently with garlic, salt, pepper. After 10 mins. remove, and fry steak quickly 1 min. each side in frying pan. Pour tomatoes over and simmer 10 mins. If meat still feels tough, go on longer, but don't raise your hopes too high. (25 mins.)

## Mushroom Beef (not quick, but dead easy)

¼ lb. braising steak     1 packet frozen *or* 1 small
1 can condensed mushroom     tin peas
  soup     oil, salt, pepper, herbs

Cut skin and excess fat off meat, and cut into two or three pieces. Beat. Fry quickly on all sides in oil. Add peas, soup, flavourings, and simmer very gently 40 mins. (You can add potatoes that have been boiled for ten minutes beforehand; or eat it with instant potato.) (50 mins.)

## Creole Beef (this also works with rabbit)

| | |
|---|---|
| ¼ lb. braising steak | 2 tomatoes, *or* squeeze of |
| 1 pimento | tomato paste |
| 1 onion | oil, salt, pepper, herbs |
| 1 small tin sweetcorn (*or* a | |
| few half cooked potatoes) | |

Cut skin and excess fat off beef and cut up into several pieces; beat them; fry them in oil on all sides and remove from pan. Chop onion and pimento, fry 5 mins. Put back beef, add everything else, and simmer gently ½ hour or more. You can substitute half cooked potatoes for the sweet corn; or eat it with rice as a variation (see page 78). (¾ hr.)

## Hamburgers

| | |
|---|---|
| ¼ lb. minced beef | flour (optional) |
| 1 onion (optional) | egg (optional) |
| herbs, salt, pepper | 2 large soft round rolls |

The classic hamburger is just a flat patty of mince fried quickly in very little, very hot fat. For this, frozen steakettes and the like are excellent. A slightly tastier hamburger is made by frying an onion and mixing it and the meat with egg and herbs, and dusting the patty with flour before frying. Traditionally served in a toasted bun with a lot of tomato ketchup. And some raw onion, if you are alone and want to stay that way. (10 mins.)

## Cheeseburger

As above, but a square of cheese goes on top when you have turned it over after frying first side. (10 mins.)

## Bœuf en Hachis (or Superhamburger)

| | |
|---|---|
| ¼ lb. minced beef | 1 slice bread, crumbled |
| 1 sausage | herbs, chopped garlic (optional) |
| 1 onion | salt, pepper |

Fry onion first; then mix all together; form flat patties and cook in real butter 5 mins. each side. (15 mins.)

## *Chilli con Carne* (two helpings)

| | |
|---|---|
| ¼ lb. minced beef | pinch chilli powder (essential) |
| 1 tin baked beans | oil |
| 1 onion (optional) | |

Open the beans. Fry the chopped onion; add juice poured from beans and the chilli powder. Stir. Add the mince, breaking it up with a spoon and stirring till no more red is visible (don't go on too long). Add beans, stir, simmer 5 mins. on low gas. (More simmering-time improves it.) (15 mins.)

## *Corned Beef Hash*

| | |
|---|---|
| ½ tin corned beef | 1 onion |
| 2 or 3 cooked potatoes (or instant potato) | salt, pepper |
| | herbs |

Chop the onion fine and fry it in oil. Meanwhile mix corned beef, herbs, potatoes, salt, pepper, and a little milk or water. When onion is cooked (10 mins.) add mixture, leave on lowest gas till brown underneath – say 5 mins. Turn out like an omelette. (15 mins.)

Green salad is the best accompaniment to this.

(For the other half of the corned beef tin, you could try risotto, Broken Meat Salad, or fritters as on page 116.)

## *Stew* (two helpings at least)

| | |
|---|---|
| ½ lb. stewing beef | ½ teaspoon meat extract |
| 3 potatoes | ½ teaspoon mustard (preferably |
| 3 onions | French) |
| 3 carrots | herbs, salt, pepper; garlic (optional) |
| 2 leeks and/or | flour |
| 1 turnip (optional) | fat for *Method 1* |

*Method 1.* Prepare meat by cutting off all the nasty bits and beating a large teaspoon of flour into it (if you can't be bothered, O K – but the meat may be a bit tough). In any

case *roll* the meat in flour. Heat a little fat in saucepan, and turn the bits in it until brown on all sides. Remove; fry chopped onion for 5 mins. Add everything, including the meat extract dissolved in one small cup water. Simmer as slowly as possible on asbestos for 2 hrs.

'A stew boiled is a stew spoiled' is not altogether true, but if you can keep it just below boiling point it will be better.

*Method 2.* Prepare meat as above but without flour. Put meat and chopped vegetables in pan with small cup water, meat extract, seasonings; bring to boil; reduce gas as low as it will go, and simmer 2 hrs. Not less than 15 mins. before the end, put one tablespoon flour into a cup, mix with some liquid from pan, and stir back into stew.

This method is less trouble than the other, but makes a paler and, to my mind, slightly less succulent stew.

## Split Pea Stew (two helpings)

| | |
|---|---|
| ½ lb. stewing beef | oil |
| 4 onions | lemon juice; tomato paste |
| ½ cup split peas (the green ones give a better appearance) | salt, pepper; parsley (optional) |

Start off exactly as for stew *method 1*; when you have browned the meat in the oil, add everything else and a cupful of water. Simmer 2 hrs; add more water if necessary. (2¼ hrs.)

## Pot Roast

I am hardly supposing that you will start pot-roasting on an ordinary evening home from the office, but if some week-end you get a nostalgic urge for a good hunk of meat just like mother used to give you, here's how. (A *heavy* saucepan is essential.)

| | |
|---|---|
| small joint of beef (about 2 lb.) | 4 carrots |
| 4 medium potatoes | 1 tablespoon flour |
| 4 onions | salt, pepper |
| | fat |

84

Wipe joint (*don't* wash it) and dust it all over with flour. If you like garlic, stick several cloves of it down between the fat and the lean, and to hell with nostalgia for Ye Olde Englishe. Heat a little fat in the biggest and heaviest saucepan you can lay hands on; turn the joint on all sides to brown. Add vegetables, and put on lowest possible gas on asbestos with lid on for $1\frac{1}{2}$ hours or more. ($1\frac{3}{4}$ hrs minimum.)

Use the left-over meat in a substantial salad; with spaghetti; in a risotto; in stuffed cabbage leaves, stuffed tomatoes, stuffed pimentoes; or add to a tinned or packet soup.

(This can also be made with rabbit.)

## VEAL

Veal should be a delicate pale pink; the darker it is, the tougher. Lovely pale escalopes are expensive, but they beat out in no time to more than twice their original size, so you do not need as much as you might think. The cheaper cuts of veal take a long, long time to cook; but you can often buy veal mince, which you can deal with more quickly. As veal is commoner on the Continent than here, there are plenty of stylish recipes for it which I have included in the other section. Wiener Schnitzel is here not because it is not good enough for company but because it is so beautifully quick and easy as well. The test of a good Wiener Schnitzel, it is alleged, was that the Viennese could sit on it without making a grease-mark on their trousers – so don't have too much fat in the pan.

### Wiener Schnitzel

| | |
|---|---|
| 1 small escalope of veal | breadcrumbs |
| 1 egg | lemon |

Beat out the escalope till it is thin and twice as broad as it was. Beat egg lightly on plate; spread breadcrumbs on another. Dip veal first in egg, then in breadcrumbs; fry in hot oil or butter for $1\frac{1}{2}$ mins. each side. You can fry potatoes first (and add 10–15 mins. to timing); but this is lovely with just a squeeze of lemon juice.

You can dip it in flour instead of crumbs, but it is not quite so good. (7 mins. – more if you have to make breadcrumbs first.)


## Fricassée of Veal

¼ lb. veal mince  
1 tin condensed mushroom soup

1 tin peas and/or 2 or 3 cooked potatoes or ½ cup cooked rice

Heat fat in frying pan; add veal mince. Break it down rapidly with a spoon till none of it shows pink any more; add soup; stir; add your pre-cooked vegetable – rice, potatoes, peas, or whatever it is. (5 mins. – or 25 if you have to cook the rice.)


## Veal Rissoles and Potatoes

¼ lb. veal mince  
2 or 3 potatoes  
1 egg

1 onion  
parsley, salt, pepper  
butter or oil

Chop potatoes into thin chips and fry in butter with onion. When onion is fairly soft (say after 7 mins.) remove it, while potatoes go on cooking, and mix it with everything else. Form into flat rissoles and cook gently with the potatoes for 5 mins. each side. (20 mins.)


## Tomato Veal Chop

1 veal cutlet  
3 tomatoes

1 onion  
garlic, salt, pepper

Stick little pieces of garlic into the veal; turn it 1 min. each side in hot oil or butter; add chopped onions and tomatoes and simmer very gently 20 mins. or until tender. (25 mins.)

## Sauté of Veal (two helpings)

| | |
|---|---|
| ½ lb. cheap veal | ¼ lb. mushrooms (optional) *or* |
| 3 chopped onions | 1 aubergine (optional) |
| 1 rasher bacon | 1 teaspoon herbs, salt, pepper |
| 2 tomatoes (optional) | butter or oil |

Chop veal into chunks and remove any wispy bits of skin.
Turn on all sides in a little hot fat in a saucepan; add onions;
fry *gently* 5 mins. Add vegetables, flavouring, and ½ cup
water, and simmer 1 hr.

If you want to add potatoes, they can sit on top of the veal
and cook in the steam. This one has a thin sauce; if you want
to mix in a dessertspoon of flour near the end (mixing it first
in cup with some of the liquid), it's OK by me. (1¼ hrs.)

## LAMB AND MUTTON

Lamb chops are second only to baked beans as the staple
food of people who live in bedsitters. Fried fast by the
hungry, they are nearly always tough; but they have the un-
deniable advantage of being unmessy and easy to recognize
and handle. Knowing the tendency we all have to go into the
butcher's with high ambitions and come out with lamb
chops, I have put in several recipes for varying their cooking; but there *are* other pieces of sheep, even if a good leg of
lamb is a bit beyond the scope of a gas ring.

It will be noted that there is no recipe for Irish Stew. I am
told that the reason I detest it is because I do not make it
properly. Possibly. But let other pens dwell on guilt and
misery, as Jane Austen said; I still maintain that almost any
other way of eating mutton is nicer.

*If you can possibly leave lamb chops in a marinade overnight*
(see page 24), *they improve 100 per cent.*

## Lamb Chops and Fried Potatoes (traditional)

| | | |
|---|---|---|
| 2 lamb chops | 2 potatoes | 1 tomato (optional) |

Heat oil or butter in frying pan to medium heat; start off

with the potatoes, cut in thin slices. When they have had
five minutes, add the chops, which you may have rubbed
with garlic or pepper, but NOT SALT. Turn up the gas, fry
quickly on each side for 1 min., then lower the gas and cook
on lower flame for 10–15 mins. depending on thickness of
chops. Add tomato 5 mins. before the end. (25 mins.)

## Lamb Chops and Cheese

2 lamb chops
1 dessertspoon grated cheese
   mixed with ½ slice crumbled bread

1 egg
1 packet frozen peas (the
   nicest accompaniment)
fat for frying

Cook frozen peas in boiling salted water as instructed on
packet. Meanwhile beat egg slightly on plate; dip chops in it,
and then in grated cheese mixture, then again in egg. Remove
peas. Fry chops gently 7 mins. each side, scooping cheese
mixture back on to chops if it falls off. Drain on clean newspaper 2 mins. while peas quickly reheat. (20 mins. by itself,
30 mins. with peas.)

## Lamb Chops and Tomato

2 lamb chops
1 large onion
½ can condensed tomato soup
2 tablespoons rice

garlic (optional), bay leaf
   (optional), salt, pepper
flour
oil for frying

Dip chops in flour; fry 1 min. each side in hot fat. Turn
down gas to medium; add finely chopped onion and fry 5
mins. Add rice; turn in fat until transparent. Add soup,
flavourings, and two tablespoons water. Simmer gently
about ½ hr or till chops are tender. Add more water if it looks
dry. (40 mins. approximately.)

## Lamb Tomato Quickie

2 lamb chops
½ can condensed tomato soup
fat for frying

2 cooked potatoes or ½
   cup cooked rice (op-
   tional)

Cut lean meat off chops and cut it into little cubes or strips. Fry very quickly until brown, turning constantly. Add soup and rice or potatoes; stir; and eat. (10 mins.)

## Lamb or Mutton Cutlets Champvallon

2 cutlets or chops of mutton or lamb
2 onions
2 sliced potatoes

garlic, herbs, salt, pepper
butter or oil
flour

Dust cutlets with flour; fry 2 mins. each side in saucepan – in butter, if possible. Remove. Fry chopped onions and potatoes cut into thin slices, hard, for 5 mins. with lid on. Lower the heat, put back chops, add garlic, salt, pepper, herbs, 2 tablespoons water (hot for choice). Put a lid on and simmer very gently $\frac{1}{2}$ hr on asbestos mat. (45 mins.)

## Lamb and Cabbage

2 lamb chops or $\frac{1}{4}$ lb. mutton
fat

$\frac{1}{2}$ cabbage
salt, pepper, herbs

Cut fat and bone off lamb or mutton; fry quickly 2 mins. each side in a little fat in saucepan. Cut cabbage in shreds; turn in fat also. Add salt, pepper, herbs; cover; cook very gently on asbestos mat 40 mins. or more. If you think this looks a bit greasy, you can shake in a level dessertspoon of flour 15 mins. before the end, mixing thoroughly. (55 mins.)

## Mutton Rissoles

$\frac{1}{4}$ lb. minced mutton
1 egg
1 onion
tomato paste or 1 peeled tomato

1 slice crumbled bread
salt, pepper, herbs
(optional)
plenty of fat for frying

Chop onion very fine; mix everything together thoroughly; add a little water if it seems dry. If you have enough fat for deep frying, form into balls and drop them into it when it is smoking hot – fry 5 mins. If not, form into flat cakes and cook 4 mins. each side in shallow fat. Eat with pre-cooked potatoes or rice (see page 78) or a tinned vegetable that will heat while the rissoles drain on clean newspaper. (10–15 mins.)

## Haricot Mutton (a good cheap filler for the week-end; two helpings at least)

½ lb. scrag end of mutton or other cheap mutton

1 onion, 1 turnip, 1 carrot, all chopped (or 2 carrots, no turnip)

1 cup haricot beans (*soaked overnight*)

flour

fat for frying

meat extract (optional)

bay leaf, herbs, salt, pepper, garlic (optional)

Trim mutton, removing the bits you are unlikely to eat. Fry mutton pieces a minute each side in a little fat in a saucepan. Remove pan from gas, and stir a dessertspoon of flour into the fat. Add everything else with a small cup of water. Simmer very gently on asbestos for 1½ hrs at least with lid on. Add a little more water if it gets dry, but it will be more likely to get sloppy. If it does, continue cooking with lid off. (2 hrs.)

## PORK

The pig contributes more to bedsitter life by way of bacon and sausages than as straight pork; but often enough there are those clean-looking pink chops to tempt you in the butcher's; and you can also buy a nice bit of loin of pork and casserole it deliciously. Whereas beef, veal, and lamb are often at their best if they are not cooked too much and are still pink inside, pork must always be well cooked – so it is not the quickest of meats whatever you do to it.

## Fried Pork Chop and Potatoes

2 or 3 potatoes

1 large pork chop

butter or oil for frying (or bacon fat)

Slice potatoes thinly. Heat fat in pan. Cook chop 1 min. each side on fairly high flame; then add potatoes, lower flame, and cook chop 10 mins. each side. (25 mins.)

## Braised Pork Chop and Celery

| | |
|---|---|
| 1 large pork chop | fat for frying |
| 1 head celery *or* 1 tin celery | salt, pepper |

Heat fat in saucepan; cook chop quickly 1 min. each side; lower gas to lowest possible and cook very gently with lid on for 45 mins. Add raw celery when you lower the gas, or tinned celery without liquid 10 mins. before the end. (50 mins.)

## Italian Pork Chops (two helpings)

| | |
|---|---|
| 2 pork chops | breadcrumbs *or* sliced potatoes |
| 1 pimento | (optional) |
| 1 tin sweetcorn | oil, salt, pepper, garlic |
| 1 onion (optional) | |

Heat fat in saucepan; turn chops 1 min. each side. Add onion (chopped), sweetcorn (with liquid from tin), pimento (chopped and seeds etc. removed). Simmer very gently 1 hr or till chops are tender. (1 hr 10 mins. approximately.)

## German Pork

| | |
|---|---|
| 1 pork chop *or* piece of loin, about ¼ lb. *after boning* | a few caraway seeds (optional) |
| 1 small tin sauerkraut | salt, pepper |
| 2 tablespoons sour cream | |

Put pork, sauerkraut, and flavourings in saucepan and cook gently for 45 mins. Stir in sour cream at the last minute. If you use loin, it will take longer. (45 mins.)

# CHICKEN

*Give me a bread and butter woman*
*I mean the real domestic kind*
*Whose heart-beat will quicken*
*On half a boiled chicken . . .*

Chicken is a word that still has a faint air of extravagance about it; but in fact chickens are now being reared so fast and furiously that they are often cheaper than good meat. This has been the case in America for years, as the rhyme shows; from America, too, come some of the best ideas for cooking chickens not so much in whole as in part. Unless you were planning to use the beak and giblets for a complicated soup, there is nothing especially reckless about buying your chicken in hunks, either fresh or frozen; and it certainly saves a lot of medieval scenes with the guts and claws. Boiling chicken is cheaper – but not cheap enough, to my mind, to justify the extra hours you have to spend cooking it.

## Fried Chicken

| | |
|---|---|
| 1 piece of chicken | flour |
| 2 potatoes, cut into small chips | salt and pepper |
| butter or oil (or a mixture) | |

Either remove the chicken skin, or leave it on but pull out anything that looks at all feathery. Add salt and pepper to a small mound of flour, and dust the chicken in it; fry it quickly all over in very hot fat. Put in the potatoes, reduce the gas, and cook gently for about 20 mins., turning occasionally. (25 mins.)

## Chicken and Celery

| | |
|---|---|
| 1 piece chicken | flour, oil, salt, pepper |
| 1 small tin celery | garlic (optional) |
| 1 egg yolk (optional) | onion (optional) |

Dust chicken; fry, as above, for a few minutes, with garlic
and chopped onion. Add celery, without its liquid. Simmer
½ hr. Stir in yolk, off the gas, just before eating. (35 mins.)

## Poule au Riz

| | |
|---|---|
| 1 piece chicken | 1 or more carrots |
| ⅓ cup rice | herbs, salt, pepper, bay leaf, garlic |
| 1 onion | (optional) |

Remove chicken skin or any stray feathers. Put everything
in pan with just enough water to cover; simmer 40 mins.
with lid on. (Add more water if it looks like drying up.) If
you use boiling chicken, boil it by itself for 1 hr first. (45
mins.)

(*There are a number of chicken casseroles in Part Two which
can easily be adapted for one or two by cutting down the
quantities.*)

## FISH

There are two schools of thought about fish. One likes to
have all the bits sold with the fish – prawns in their shells,
herrings with their heads on – so that delicious stock can be
made with these charming remains: I remember a Finnish
friend making a terrible fuss in the supermarket because she
could not buy fish-heads to make fish-head soup. For the
rest of us, however, raw fish is quite unpleasant enough
even *after* the guts and fins have been removed; and in a
bedsitter there are really no facilities for making proper use
of the bits you cannot eat.

For this reason, tinned and frozen fish – especially frozen
– is an excellent bet. One small packet of frozen fish makes
an ample meal for one: cod, herring, and haddock are the
cheapest, but sole and plaice are so nice that all you need to
buy with them is a piece of lemon and some breadcrumbs.
Unfreeze frozen fish in *cold* water – if you hold it under a hot
tap, little bits will cook in the hot water and flake off.

Tunnyfish, sild, sardines, pilchards, and herring roes are all reliable in tins; tinned salmon is nice only if it is expensive, but tinned crab is often good, though not specially cheap; tinned dressed crab spread, at a shilling is excellent value.

The smell of cooking fish is not usually too bad: it is the smell of uncooked fish about to go bad that is really unpleasant. So if it smells strongly in the shop, don't buy it – it will smell a lot worse once you get it home. And if a fish has a listless eye and looks jaded and old, it *is* old – don't let the fishmonger put you off with a lot of stuff about it being fresh up from Yarmouth this morning. Too many of them take the line that if the fish isn't fresh, you should have bought it last week when it *was* fresh.

## Fish and Chips

1 small packet frozen cod    flour; fat for frying
2 or 3 potatoes    lemon (optional)

Peel and cut up potatoes thinly *and dry them*. Fry in as much hot fat as you can for 10 mins. Meanwhile unfreeze fish; dry; roll in flour (or egg and breadcrumbs, if you have them). When chips are nearly done, move to edge of frying pan and fry fish 3 mins. each side. Drain on newspaper. (25 mins.)

(If you like fish in batter, as served in fish-and-chip shops, see page 114.)

## Mustard Sild

1 tin Norway sild    1 dessertspoon flour
1 large teaspoon French or small    1 small cup milk
   teaspoon English mustard    toast
   1 teaspoon butter

Melt butter in pan; stir in flour; gradually add liquid from tin, and milk and mustard. When it is thick, add fish and heat for 10 mins. (15 mins.)

## Cod and Onions

| | |
|---|---|
| 1 small packet frozen cod *or* one good-sized cod fillet | 1 dessertspoon flour |
| 2 large onions | herbs, salt, pepper |
| | fat |

Put cod (already thawed) in cold water and bring to boil; boil 5 mins. Remove. In other saucepan (or same, after removing fish and water into bowl) fry chopped onions in fat until golden – 7 mins. Add flour; blend in a cupful of liquid from cod; add salt, pepper, herbs. Simmer 10 mins. Add cod to re-heat. (30 mins.)

## Mediterranean Fish

| | |
|---|---|
| 1 small packet cod, haddock, whiting | herbs, salt, pepper, |
| 1 onion | parsley if pos- |
| 2 tomatoes | sible, garlic |
| lemon juice | oil for frying |

Chop onion finely, and fry with chopped garlic and parsley in olive oil. When onions are soft, add quartered tomatoes; fry for a few minutes; add 3 tablespoons water, a good squeeze of lemon juice, herbs, seasonings, and the fish. Simmer gently till fish is tender – 15 mins.

If you leave out the lemon juice, garlic, and parsley it will be all right, but not Mediterranean. As it stands, it is my favourite fish dish. (25 mins.)

## Cod and Potatoes Auvergnat

| | |
|---|---|
| 1 small packet or 1 fillet cod | parsley and/or chives, salt, |
| 2 or 3 potatoes, halved | pepper |
| butter | top of the milk or cream |

Put the peeled and halved potatoes to boil in salted water; 5 mins. after they boil, add cod; 10 mins. later, pour off water; heat a nut of butter in frying pan, add cod and potatoes; fry for a few minutes; add herbs, parsley, and top of the milk. So much less dreary than just plain boiled cod. (25 mins.)

## Devilled Soft Roes

| | |
|---|---|
| 1 tin soft roes | Worcester sauce |
| mustard (French or English) | salt, pepper |
| lemon | |

Mix mustard with sauce, salt, and pepper on plate. Dip roes in it. Fry 2 mins. each side. Eat with toast and squeezed lemon. (7 mins.)

## Soft Roes and Rice

| | |
|---|---|
| ⅓ cup rice | 1 tin condensed mushroom soup |
| 1 tin soft roes | |
| water, salt | |

Boil rice (method 1, p. 78) in salted water 12 mins. after it boils. Pour off water. Add roes and condensed soup. Stir 3 mins. while it heats. Do not boil, or soup will get too liquid. (20 mins.)

## Saucepan Fish Pie

| | |
|---|---|
| 1 small packet frozen fish (any kind) or 1 tin tunny fish | parsley, salt, pepper |
| | grated cheese (optional) |
| 2 or 3 potatoes | 1 teaspoon butter, 1 dessert-spoon flour, 1 cup milk |

Peel and slice potatoes and put on to boil in salted water. 5 mins. after they boil, add cod. Boil 10 mins. or till soft. Remove. In other saucepan (or same saucepan, after removing contents into bowl) melt butter; stir in flour, gradually add milk. When it thickens, simmer 10 mins. then put in cod and potato, add parsley, stir. Sprinkle with grated cheese. (35 mins.)

You can add a large teaspoon of mustard instead of parsley and grated cheese, in which case you have a mustard pie.

## Basque Sardines

| | |
|---|---|
| 1 tin sardines | 1 small tin peppers *or* 1 fresh |
| 1 onion | pimento (optional) |
| 2 tomatoes | salt, pepper |
| grated cheese (optional) | |

Fry chopped onion and pimento (if using fresh pimento) in oil from sardine tin. When brown, add quartered tomatoes, fish, salt, and pepper. Fry 5 mins. Shake over grated cheese. Fry 3 mins. more. (15 mins.)

## Herrings and Potatoes

| | |
|---|---|
| 2 herrings | flour, or oatmeal, or an egg and a |
| 2 cooked potatoes | spoonful of breadcrumbs |
| fat for frying | |

Make sure the fishmonger has removed head and guts –or unfreeze frozen herrings *and dry them* (or they will sputter in the fat). Dip them in the flour, or the oatmeal, or the egg and then the breadcrumbs. Fry herrings and potatoes in medium hot fat for 5 mins. each side. (15 mins.)

## Haddock Monte Carlo

| | |
|---|---|
| 1 packet frozen haddock | top of the milk |
| 2 tomatoes *or* 1 tin condensed tomato | herbs, pepper, |
|   soup | lemon juice |
| ⅓ cup rice | (optional) |
| butter | |

Put everything but the fish into a pan, and cook it for 10 mins. If real tomatoes are being used, add 3 tablespoons water. Add fish, and if necessary more water, and cook another 15 mins. (25 mins.)

## Fried Sole or Plaice

| | |
|---|---|
| 1 packet frozen sole *or* | flour or egg and breadcrumbs |
|   plaice, *or* 2 fillets | butter (if possible) |
| ½ lemon | |

Unfreeze fish completely, and dry it. Dip in flour, or in beaten egg and then breadcrumbs. Fry in medium hot butter 3 mins. each side. Squeeze lemon juice over, and chopped parsley if you happen to have it. Too good to muck about with other vegetables. (10 mins.)

## Sea Risotto (two helpings)

| | |
|---|---|
| 1 tin tunnyfish | herbs, salt, pepper, lemon |
| 1 small pot, packet, or tin | juice |
| prawns | ½ cup rice |
| 1 pimento | oil |
| 1 onion | butter |

Heat up some water in the kettle and when it boils remove and put on saucepan containing onion, oil, pimento. Fry 5 mins. Add rice. Turn until transparent. Add 1½ cups warm water from kettle, salt, pepper, and any liquid from tin of tunny. Boil gently 20 mins. Add fish, prawns, herbs, lemon juice. Heat 3 mins. Stir in spoonful of butter if possible. See also page 74. (35 mins.)

## Austrian Fish Stew (two helpings)

| | |
|---|---|
| 3 onions | sour cream or |
| 1 packet frozen haddock, cod, or fillets | milk |
| 4 potatoes | salt, pepper; oil |
| paprika (essential) | |

Chop onions fine. Fry 5 mins. in oil. Add fish, potatoes very thinly sliced, ½ cup water, salt, pepper, 1 teaspoon or more paprika. Simmer ½ hour. Stir in a tablespoonful sour cream or sour milk. (40 mins.)

## Jamaican Spiced Fish Cakes

| | |
|---|---|
| 1 small packet or ¼ lb. cod | 1 green chilli pepper, or 1 |
| 1 onion | small pimento and a pinch |
| 1 tomato | of chilli powder |
| flour; fat | |

Drop cod into saucepan of water and boil 10 mins. Chop up very fine the onion, tomato, chilli pepper or pimento. Mix cod with this, and shape into flat cakes. Dust in flour and fry in hot fat 4 mins. each side. (20 mins.)

## Hot Buttered Crab

| | |
|---|---|
| 1 tin crab or ¼ lb. fresh crab | pepper |
| 1 dessertspoon breadcrumbs *or* crumbled bread | butter (a dessertspoon at least) |
| parsley | toast |
| lemon juice and/or vinegar | |

Melt butter and add crab and everything else. Stir. Heat 3 mins. Pile on toast. Nice with a green-and-cucumber salad. (5 mins.)

## Kedgeree

| | |
|---|---|
| ½ cup any cooked fish – haddock is traditional (*or* small tin tunnyfish or salmon) | 1 egg |
| | butter |
| 1 cup *cooked* rice | lemon juice |

First hard-boil the egg – 10 mins. Then put as much butter as you can spare into a saucepan, heat, add fish, rice, lemon juice, and the egg (chopped). Heat for a few minutes and eat. (15 mins.)

## Scallops

2 scallops    1 potato    parsley

Get the fishmonger to remove everything from scallops but red and white flesh. Slice potatoes thinly. Fry together *very gently* in butter for 15 mins. Sprinkle with parsley. (20 mins.)

## Fish in Sauce Lyall

| | |
|---|---|
| 1 small packet or 2 fillets any fish | 1 dessertspoon bottled mayonnaise or salad cream |
| 1 teaspoon butter | |
| 1 dessertspoon flour | |
| 1 teaspoonful vinegar | 1 teaspoonful mustard |
| | 1 small cup of milk |

Make a white sauce, as on page 42. Add salad cream, mustard, vinegar, pepper, and fish (from which any dark skin has been removed). Simmer very gently for 20 mins. (25 mins.)

## CURRY

Curry finds itself in this section because it is useless to try to impress anyone with a curry nowadays unless you have spent several years out East and are prepared to talk about it, as well as cook, for hours on end. When it comes to really elaborate curries it is much better to be on the receiving end, and fortunately most people who live in bedsitters know at least one Indian or Pakistani who is delighted to make a curry for an admiring friend. Moreover, they are apt to know their proportions only in terms of ·01 grains of saffron per half sheep, so that they will often make enough curry for you and everyone on the staircase to feed off for a week.

However, here is an unassuming straightforward curry that will work on meat, fish, or any odds and ends you happen to have over.

## *Curry for Meat, Fish, Rabbit, or Leftovers*

| | |
|---|---|
| 2 onions | 2 teaspoons curry powder |
| 2 tomatoes (*or* squeeze of tomato paste) | ¼ lb. meat or fish or mince |
| | 1 dessertspoon flour |
| 1 teaspoon meat extract dissolved in 1 cup water | fat for frying |

Fry onions gently for 5 mins. Add tomatoes and flour; stir. Add meat-extract and water; stir. Add curry powder and KEEP THE GAS LOW AT THIS POINT (too much direct heat seems to burn off the *taste* of the curry and leave only the *sting* – if this happens, add more curry, if you can bear to). Add meat or rabbit and simmer 1 hr. If fish, add after ½ hr. (1¼ hrs.)

This is even better if you let it get cold and then heat it up.

## Curried Eggs (a dish of even less oriental splendour than the last one)

| | |
|---|---|
| 2 or more eggs | 1 small cup milk and water |
| 1 teaspoon butter | onion (optional) |
| 1 dessertspoon flour | 1 large teaspoon curry powder |

Boil eggs for 7 mins. Peel and halve them. Make white sauce with butter, flour, and milk-and-water; stir in curry powder and cook GENTLY for 10 mins. Add eggs to reheat; dish up and eat. You can fry the onion at the beginning of the sauce, and blend the flour into the fat-and-onion instead of into the fat alone. (25 mins.)

## Curried Omelette (cheating)

| | |
|---|---|
| 1 small tin curried beans | 2 eggs |

Heat beans in small pan. Make omelette, as on page 59, and pour beans on top before removing omelette from pan. (10 mins.)

(See also CURRIED MACARONI, page 75, and CURRY SALAD, page 108.)

## Curry Rice

Curries should have rice with them. The best way is to make it beforehand and warm it up in a bowl, with a very little water, on top of the saucepan in which the curry is cooking. (Or use pre-cooked 'Momento' instant rice – if you know where to buy it.)

Alternatively, you can keep the curry simmering on top of the rice, if you cook the rice by a fast-boiling method instead of a slow simmering one (see page 78).

Tinned curries can be heated up over a pan of cooking rice.

********************************

CHAPTER 6

# Salads and Sandwiches

## SALADS

PEOPLE in bedsitters have more need of a good range of salads than most, since they are inevitably right in among their cooking and to heat the gas ring at all is unbearable on a really warm day. Lush and frequent salads, too, help to counteract that sinking feeling that goes with living in a bedsitter. I mean the feeling that all these baked beans, etc., can't really be *healthy*. I have dealt with four main types of salad food here: the straight mixture of cold vegetables and a sauce; the substantial salad which is a meal in itself; cold salad foods which make a good dinner-party first course or a party snack; and sandwiches. (Hot sandwiches are in the Snacks section. This may seem illogical, but you just don't look under salads if your stomach is grinding for a good warm snack.)

But before we begin, there is the question of salad dressing. Here are three: the standard *French dressing* which goes perfectly with anything that will grow south of the Loire – lettuce, tomatoes, olives, leeks, aubergines, avocadoes; *mayonnaise*, which is best when you are eating cold meat, fish, or chicken; a *Scandinavian cream dressing* for a change, which is nice with things like grated cabbage or carrot.

## French Dressing

| | |
|---|---|
| 2 tablespoons oil (olive oil for choice) | ½ teaspoon French mustard (or less English mustard) |
| 1 tablespoon vinegar (wine vinegar for choice) | ¼ teaspoon salt<br>sprinkling of pepper |

Mix all this together just before tossing your lettuce in it or pouring it over the tomatoes. Use less vinegar, and/or a $\frac{1}{4}$ teaspoon sugar, if this is too acid for your taste. It pays to make up a large quantity of this and keep it in a bottle, giving it a really good shake before using. It will not go bad.

## Mayonnaise

A lot of unnecessary fuss is made about this: it is not as difficult as people make out. And it completely transforms a cold meat or fish meal. You need

1 egg yolk
1–3 teaspoons lemon juice (or vinegar) to taste

salt, pepper, $\frac{1}{4}$ teaspoon French mustard
up to 1 cup olive oil

Beat the egg yolk first by itself, in a bowl for choice (gripped between your knees is easiest – leaves one hand free for pouring). You can make this in a cup, but it's rather a wearing job that way. Then add the olive oil ONE DROP AT A TIME TO BEGIN WITH, stirring hard throughout. No kidding: you *must* do it this way. After a few minutes you can increase the oil to a tiny trickle, but keep stirring all the time. When you have as much as you want (and one egg yolk will take in a phenomenal amount of oil), add your seasonings and vinegar or lemon juice. If at any point it does look like curdling, add it gradually to another egg yolk with tremendous beatings.

One is always told that if you stir it the wrong way round, or the egg is too cold or too hot, or the wind is in the east, or you forget to say your prayers, all will be lost. I can only say that this has never, touch wood, happened to me, though just about every other known cooking accident has.

## Scandinavian Cream Dressing

1 carton single cream
1 teaspoon vinegar (or less)

$\frac{1}{4}$ teaspoon French mustard
1 teaspoon sugar

Beat all together and eat with shredded cabbage, carrots, peas, etc.

## Lettuce Salad

Wash lettuce, shaking each leaf under tap. If you have a bowl, rub it round with garlic; make a French dressing; dump the shaken lettuce on top, and only toss it together thoroughly when you are just about to eat it.

## Salade de Tomates

Sliced tomatoes with a French dressing and a little finely chopped onion and/or chives sprinkled over. Make up an hour beforehand if possible. Chopped parsley makes it perfect.

## Potato Salad

Potatoes, boiled in their jackets to save trouble, peeled, and with a French dressing (and chopped chives if possible) added while they are still warm.

If you like it with a bottled mayonnaise-type salad dressing, why not buy a tin or carton or half pound of potato salad? Saves a lot of trouble.

## Spring Salad

Sliced cucumber and watercress, if possible spring onions, with or without lettuce, thoroughly washed. A French dressing goes well with this. Watercress has more essential vitamins than lettuce, I am told. If you care.

## Raw Mushroom Salad

Choose nice-looking white mushrooms; wash, drain, and slice, but do not peel unless any are exceptionally rough. Pour over a French dressing, if possible half an hour before you are going to eat.

## Canadian Salad

Two tomatoes and an orange sliced up and covered with a
dessertspoon of tomato ketchup mixed with a little of the
orange juice.

## Arabian Salad

An orange, sliced; an onion, sliced; 4 stoned black olives;
salt, pepper, and a little olive oil. Let this stand ½ hour at
least, if possible.

## Cabbage Salad

Shred a quarter of a cabbage, a carrot or two, and an apple,
with a few raisins (optional). Mix with mayonnaise (bottled
or real) or Scandinavian cream dressing.

## Avocado Pear

Nicest of all simply with a French dressing. Alternatively,
take out the flesh, mix with a chopped onion, 2 chopped
tomatoes; and a dash of paprika (optional). Eat this with a
lettuce and some French dressing.

## Royal Slaw

Shred some red cabbage, 2 sliced sticks of celery, a sliced
peeled apple, and a banana. Soak in a French dressing, or
serve with a cream dressing.

## Aubergine Salad (this is lovely, but actually *not* for a hot day)

Boil an aubergine for 15 mins. Remove flesh from skin, and
pound it with a little crushed garlic and some salt and
pepper. Gradually beat in 3 dessertspoons olive oil; and add
a squeeze of lemon juice at the end.

*Norwegian Cucumber Salad* (sour and bracing; goes
 well with fish)

Slice a cucumber; sprinkle with salt and pepper and a teaspoon of vinegar or lemon juice. Chop some chives; mix
with sour cream and pour over cucumber.

## MORE SUBSTANTIAL SALADS

### Creole Salad

A packet of prawns, a hard-boiled egg (optional, if you can't
face boiling it), a small tin of potato salad or some cold
potatoes mixed with French dressing.

### Fish Salad

As above, but with tinned tunny fish instead of prawns.

### Genoese Salad (an hors d'œuvre)

A few slices of salami, a lump of salted cream cheese, and
either a few sticks of celery or some stoned black olives. No
dressing needed.

### Salade Niçoise

One of the most blissful salads there is. A meal for you, or a
first course for guests.

One lettuce, 2 tomatoes, half a dozen stoned black olives,
a few anchovies (keep the rest of the tin for anchovy toast),
a chopped green pimento. French dressing with, if anything,
extra vinegar; and if it's your main dish, add tunny fish as
well.

### Salade à l'Île Barbe

Cooked potatoes, a small tin cooked peppers, some chopped-
up ham; a few mushrooms and/or some lobster or crawfish;
a few olives; French dressing. A complete and luscious meal.

## Corned Beef Slaw

Half a tin of corned beef, a shredded carrot, some shredded cabbage, and if possible a little pickle of some kind. Bought mayonnaise with an extra teaspoon of oil and of vinegar added, and garlic. Mix all together.

## French Beans and Tunny Salad

Cook French beans, or open and slightly heat a tin (*not* so nice). Add French dressing while still warm; arrange tunny fish pieces on it.

## Portuguese Salad (good for entertaining: you can do it the day before)

Mix cold cooked rice, a couple of hard-boiled eggs, some chopped-up tomatoes, a chopped-up raw pepper or two (minus seeds), and perhaps a little chopped ham, with a lot of French dressing for the rice to absorb. An anchovy or two, if you have them left over, would feel quite at home in this; as would a good many other scraps.

## Herring Salad

Take a couple of bought cooked herrings and some potato salad, tinned or made. Either add beetroot and some sour cream, mustard, and pepper; *or* add apple and French dressing with herbs in.

## Broken Meat Salad

You can often buy bits of ham, tongue, luncheon meat, etc., at half price because they are not in neat slices. Mix anything like this with tomato, potato salad, and if necessary extra dressing. Add herbs and parsley, and let it stand for a while if possible. Nicer still if you arrange it in layers – first potato, then meat, then tomato – or beetroot, if you prefer – then more meat, etc.

## *Curry Salad* (for leftover macaroni)

Mix a little curry powder into some mayonnaise, bought or real. Add chunks of celery and a little chopped onion and mix with cold boiled macaroni. Hard-boiled eggs optional.

## COLD SALAD HORS D'ŒUVRES
which can be eaten with the fingers

### *Stuffed Tomatoes*

Cut tops off tomatoes, scoop out the pulp and mix it with:

(1) A carton of cottage cheese, some chopped-up raw pimento or shredded raw cabbage, and a small tin of tunny or salmon – not sardines.

*or*

(2) Some washed raw spinach chopped very finely and mixed with some sour cream (about one teaspoonful per tomato).

These quantities fill enough tomatoes for a first course for four to six people, using 1 lb. of tomatoes.

*or*

(3) Fill with mixture as for Portuguese Salad (above).

### *Stuffed Celery Sticks*

Wash celery, cut off tops, and divide into sticks. Mix a carton of cottage cheese, a small packet of shrimps or some shredded cabbage or some diced apple; pile the mixture on one end of each stick and dust with paprika if possible.

### *Cold Mushrooms*

Choose attractive white mushrooms all roughly the same size. Allow 4 medium ones per person. Fry them, so gently that the fat never really gets sizzling hot, for about 10 mins. Then remove them, and fry the stalks (finely chopped). To the fried stalks add chopped parsley, a teaspoon of breadcrumbs per person, some more chopped cooked mushroom if you have it left over, and some *very* finely chopped garlic. Pile this on the whole mushrooms and eat cold.

## Stuffed Eggs

Hard-boil 1 egg per person. Peel and halve lengthways. Take out yolks, and mix in a basin with a little butter or salad cream and some mustard, salt, pepper – do it by taste. Pile back on whites. Hand round on a plate with lettuce leaves on it.

## Stuffed Ham

Spread cream cheese on small slices of ham; roll up and if necessary secure with headless matchstick or toothpick.

# SANDWICHES

You can serve small open sandwiches as a first course; or eat large open sandwiches as a snack. If you are offering these to other people, it is worth while having at least two different sorts and bothering about their appearance. These, obviously, are only suggestions: the possible variations are infinite.

## Green Pea Sandwiches

Cook some peas (fresh or frozen), and drain. Mash with a fork. Beat in some cream – a carton of double cream if possible. Spread thickly on thin slices of brown bread and butter, and roll up.

## Egg and Anchovy (standard Scandinavian)

Slices of hard-boiled egg with a rolled-up anchovy on each – or in strips if you have plenty; on brown or rye bread.

## Liver Sausage and Cucumber

Spread liver sausage; lay cucumber slices on it. A radish on each improves the appearance.

## Mustard Ham (best on rye bread)

Mix a little mustard in the butter you spread on the bread, and put a little chopped apple under the ham, a very thin apple ring on top of it.

## Cream Cheese Spread

(1)

Mix chopped cucumber, cottage cheese, some chopped chives if possible, and top each sandwich with a sliced radish. If the mixture gets too stiff to spread, moisten with milk.

(2)

Cream cheese, chopped watercress, a dash of paprika if possible.

## Mock Pâté Sandwich

Liver sausage mixed with cream cheese and a little very finely chopped onion.

## Salmon and Cucumber

Spread bread with mayonnaise, lay pieces of salmon and slices of cucumber on top.

## Western Salad Sandwich

Chopped cooked bacon, celery, apple on salad dressing.

### A few hints on making ordinary sandwiches

1. Cut the bread thin, spread filling thick. The most expensive filling in the world is ruined if it is overwhelmed by bread.

2. If you possibly can, put lettuce into *any* sort of sandwich, as the Americans do, unless there is cucumber or watercress there already.

3. Either spread right out to the crusts or cut them off.

4. Wrap the sandwiches in a polythene bag to keep fresh.

5. If you are eating them at home, try toasting the bread sometimes; to my mind it makes a much nicer sandwich than untoasted bread.

✳✳✳✳✳✳✳✳✳✳✳✳✳✳✳✳✳✳✳✳✳✳✳✳✳

CHAPTER 7

# Hot Snacks and Oddments

### Cheese Steaks (the bedsitter's Welsh Rarebit)

Fry chunks of Gruyère about 2 in. square and 1 in. thick in butter at medium heat for 6–7 mins. and eat on toast. They should not melt entirely, but turn golden brown. Move them about to prevent sticking. (10 mins.)

### Scotch Woodcock

For each person, fry an egg (in butter if possible). Make toast, and while still hot spread it with anchovy paste. Top with the egg. (5 mins.)

### Cinnamon Toast

Put a lump of butter, a tablespoon of sugar, and half a teaspoon of cinnamon in a small pan. Heat it just until you can pour it, stirring hard. Spread it on toast. You can put more sugar if you like. (5 mins.)

### Hot Salmon Sandwich

Mix a little leftover salmon, a stick of chopped celery, and a teaspoon of bottled mayonnaise; cut two thin slices of bread, butter them, make the sandwich, and fry till golden brown both sides. (10 mins.)

### Croque-Monsieur

Two thin slices of bread, buttered, with a slice of ham and a slice of Gruyère cheese between, fried in medium hot fat till golden brown. (7 mins.)

## Hot Dogs

Heat up frankfurters in nearly boiling water for 5 mins. Meanwhile split and toast long-shaped soft rolls, and butter them. Shake the water off the frankfurters, spread each with a little French mustard, and eat between the rolls. (Average tin of frankfurters contains six.) (10 mins.)

## Cheese Fondue (make this for two people)

Mix 1 tablespoon butter, 2 eggs well beaten, salt, pepper, and 2 tablespoons grated cheese (preferably Gruyère, as it's a Swiss food; if you use Parmesan, use less cheese and more butter). Stir over very gentle heat till smooth, and dip pieces of toast into it. If you want to make more, you can increase the cheese, using the same number of eggs. If you are making it for company, add a small glass of white wine if you possibly can. (10 mins.)

## Cheese Balls

Mix 2 tablespoons grated cheese with 1 tablespoon flour; salt and pepper. Beat an egg and mix it in. Heat fat (deep if possible) and drop the mixture in teaspoon by teaspoon. Drain on paper. (10 mins.)

## Rum Omelette

Beat 2 eggs as for an ordinary omelette, but add a little sugar as well as salt. When cooked, remove from pan, sprinkle with sugar, pour over 2 tablespoons rum, and set it alight. (5 mins.)

## Zabaione (the best food in the world: for 2)

Three egg yolks, 3 dessertspoons sugar, and a small wine-glass Marsala (or Madeira or sherry). Beat egg yolks in bowl; add sugar; beat till light and fluffy. Add Marsala; beat. Set over a bowl of nearly boiling water and BEAT ALL THE TIME until it thickens. It should not have as pongy piece at the bottom, or curdle. It is not a custard – and not difficult, either. Eat with teaspoons from glasses. (10 mins.)

## PANCAKES AND FRITTERS

The basic batter for fritters and pancakes is the same:

| | |
|---|---|
| 1 breakfast cup flour | ½ pint milk, or milk and water |
| 1 egg | pinch of salt |

The differences are these. Pancakes are made by mixing the whole egg into the flour and gradually adding the milk, stirring out all lumps and beating hard. Fritters are made the same way, except that you keep back the egg white and beat it stiff and fold it into the mixture just before you use it – this is what makes it crisp. Although batter will keep for a day or two, this stiff egg white will subside: it follows that you can use leftover fritter batter for pancakes, but not vice versa.

With pancakes, use as little fat as you can – in fact some people just wipe the hot pan with a greased paper; with fritters, use as much as you can spare, deep frying if you can, especially for things that are round rather than flat.

One is always told that it is better for batter to stand for at least an hour between mixing and using; and so it is. But it is not *so much* the worse for being used at once that you should give up the idea of doing fritters or pancakes altogether if you have no time to let it stand. Go ahead anyway.

*Warning:* This sort of frying, especially deep frying, is smelly and hot. Make fritters for the friend across the way by all means – but don't chance it on polite company.

## PANCAKES

Have the mixture *thin*–as thin as thin cream. Thick batters make stodgy pancakes. Have the pan very hot; pour out a dollop of batter; tip it this way and that to spread it; when it is golden, turn it over carefully with the fish slice. (Toss pancakes, over your landlady's furniture? You must be crazy.)

People with two rings or a warmer can keep pancakes hot over a pan of boiling or near-boiling water – the best way, actually.

## Pancakes and Lemon

Plain pancakes, dusted with sugar, rolled up and eaten with lemon juice squeezed over them.

## Apple Pancakes

Grate, or chop very finely indeed, half an apple per pancake per person. Pour batter for pancake; sprinkle apple all over the uncooked surface. Cover with a little more batter before turning pancake to finish cooking. Dust with sugar. Do not roll.

## Stuffed Pancakes

Make a stuffing from some mince fried gently with onions; or sausage meat fried with tomatoes; or bacon and herbs and parsley fried together; or any leftovers chopped finely and heated up. Have it hot in a pan on a newspaper on the floor beside you as you cook, and put a spoonful of stuffing on each pancake before you roll it up.

## Onion Pancakes

Fry onions (perhaps with sausages); mix the onions with batter and make as above. This is ideal for using up small quantities of leftover batter – if you are making a really small one, you need not even take the sausage out of the pan.

COOKING TO STAY ALIVE

### FRITTERS

Make sure the fat is really hot – a faint smoke rising from it –
and not too high in the pan or it may bubble over. Drop the
fritters in and STAND BACK – or the fat may splash up in
your face. Fry the fritters till they are a deep golden brown;
drain on clean newspaper. Heat up fat again between batches;
and don't try to do too many at once.

## Apple Fritters

Peel and core 1 lb. cooking apples (for two) and cut into thin
rings. Dip in sugar, then in batter, and drop into fat. Drain
on clean newspaper, and sprinkle with sugar.

*Pineapple Fritters* and *Banana Fritters* are the same – you
can use tinned pineapple or fresh.

## Raisin Fritters

Mix raisins in with batter (but don't use *all* the batter till
you see how far the raisins are going to go) and drop little
dollops into the fat. Drain on clean newspaper, sprinkle with
sugar.

## Spam Fritters

Slice up a tin of spam, dip slices in batter, and fry. This one
is perfectly all right in shallow fat, provided there is plenty of
it. (You can do this with corned beef too.)

## Wiltshire Porkies

Little balls of sausage meat dipped in the batter and fried in
deep fat. Very filling.

## Scampi

At the risk of being inconsistent, I must point out that the
best batter for scampi has no egg yolk, but 3 tablespoons

olive oil instead. Otherwise it goes exactly the same as normal fritter batter. Break up the scampi (if frozen) into small pieces, pour batter in a plate; dip them into it and fry in deep fat. Eat with Tartare Sauce (page 170) or squeezed lemon.

✳✳✳✳✳✳✳✳✳✳✳✳✳✳✳✳✳✳✳✳✳✳✳✳

CHAPTER 8

# Puddings and Sweet Dishes

I HAVE not attempted to divide this chapter into cooking for yourself and cooking for company, since I believe that few people eating alone bother with *any* pudding – unless it is tinned fruit or a bought pastry. However, some of these are quite simple enough to make for yourself if you are in the mood, and there is also the possibility that you may be given fruit from the country and need to know what to do with it.

The first batch are recipes which you can eat as soon as you have made them; the rest are ones which need to be left to set or get cold.

## Apple Cream

For each person:

1 large eating apple, *or* 2 tablespoons tinned apple purée

1 dessertspoon condensed milk

Grate the apple if you have a grater, or shred it with a knife; mix with condensed milk. This *looks* most dismal, so sprinkle with cinnamon or shredded chocolate if you have any.

## Chocolate Cherry Cream

For each person:

3 chocolate biscuits
1 tablespoon whipped cream

1 tablespoon cherry jam

Break up biscuits; mix with almost all the jam and cream; leave a little of each for decorating.

## Poires Belle Hélène (for two)

| | |
|---|---|
| 1 tin pears | 1 4-oz. bar chocolate |
| 1 teaspoon butter | |

Pour off the liquid and arrange pears in bowl or in individual dishes. Melt chocolate in pan with butter and a very little of the juice; pour over pears and eat while sauce is still hot.

## Poor Knights

For each person:

| | |
|---|---|
| 1 slice of bread | 1 tablespoon jam or soft fruit |
| 1 dessertspoon cream | |

*Also*:
1 egg and some milk and butter

Beat up an egg with a tablespoon of milk (or more, if needed). Cut crusts off bread and dip each piece for a minute each side in egg mixture. Fry in butter until golden brown; lay fruit on it and top with cream. You can also eat this simply sprinkled with sugar, if you have no fruit.

## Veiled Country Lass (this is the Scandinavian name – she is perhaps better known in Britain as Cold Charlotte)

For each person:

| | |
|---|---|
| 1 small cupful breadcrumbs | 1 tin baby food apple |
| 1 tablespoon raspberry jam | purée |
| butter | cream (optional) |

Fry breadcrumbs in butter till they are crisp – a few minutes only. Make a sort of trifle with a layer of crumbs, a layer of apple, a layer of jam and so on. With cream if trying to impress; otherwise, with top of the milk.

## Raspberry Whip (expensive but a sure-fire winner: serves two)

| | |
|---|---|
| 1 packet frozen raspberries | 1 bottle double cream |
| 1 egg white (optional) | 1 or 2 dessertspoons sugar |

Beat cream, adding a little top of milk to make it go further. Crush all but a few raspberries. Beat all together. Beat egg white and fold in. Decorate with remaining raspberries.

## Strawberry Shortcake

You cannot make the shortcake yourself; but a fair approximation can be made this way.

### 'Old-fashioned' type

1 packet frozen strawberries
    (or a tin, or fresh)
double cream

1 or 2 sweet scones per
    person

Drain liquid off strawberries. Halve scones and heat them in front of fire. Spread with butter. Fill with half the strawberries, crushed. Spread the rest of strawberries on top and drench with beaten-up cream.

### Cake type

As above, but buy a sponge ring or a sponge cake. This one is usually made up in one large cake rather than individual cakes. If you buy a sponge cake with cream, you can take some of the cream from its filling to spread on top.

## Apple Cream Sponge (sounds complicated, but is easy and delicious: serves two to three)

1 lb. cooking apples *or* 2 tins
    apple baby food
sugar, if cooking apples are used

4–6 sponge fingers
2 eggs
6 tablespoons milk

Stew apples in a little water with sugar to taste; mash them up and let them cool. (Or just open tin of apple purée.) Pour half the apple over sponge, arranged in bottom of bowl or individual dishes. Make a custard with the yolks of the eggs and the milk – i.e. stir it over gentle heat till it thickens. Pour over the apples and sponge. Beat whites stiff. Mix carefully with other half of apples and put on top of custard. If you have two whites left over, you can leave out the custard altogether, though of course it is not quite so nice.

This also works well with stewed *gooseberries*, and even *rhubarb*.

## Strawberry Crunch (a good emergency pudding for two)

| | |
|---|---|
| 4 digestive biscuits | 1 small tin strawberries (or |
| cream or 1 egg white | raspberries) |

Crush biscuits to crumbs, and moisten with strawberry juice. Drain strawberries of remaining juice and lay on biscuit. Top either with cream or with beaten egg white with a few of the strawberries crushed and added after beating.

## Custard

If those who like custard with their fruit feel the custard-powder firms have had enough of their money, this is the real thing:

¼ pint milk      1 dessertspoon sugar      1 egg yolk

Beat all this together and heat it very gently, stirring, until it thickens. DO NOT BOIL. (If making larger quantities, add 1 white per 2 yolks.)

For Apple Fritters, Raisin Fritters, Pineapple Fritters, Banana Fritters and Apple Pancakes, see pages 114–17.

## Jam Fritters

bread      jam      butter

Make jam sandwiches as if you were setting out for a picnic; and fry them till golden brown on both sides.

## Fruit Waffles (hardly a recipe: merely a reminder)

| | |
|---|---|
| 1 packet frozen waffles | 1 tin fruit |
| ice cream (optional but perfect) | cream (optional) |

Toast waffles at the fire. Drain juice from tin. Heap waffle with fruit, plus cream or ice cream. The contrast between hot waffles and ice cream is nicest of all (leftover waffles can be eaten with jam, or with bacon for breakfast.)

*The following puddings all need time to set or get cold: make them the day before if you are entertaining.*

## Orange Cream (for four)

1 orange jelly      1 carton double cream      3 oranges

Make jelly as instructed on packet. Leave to cool until it is thick and beginning to set, then mix in the flesh of the oranges. Whip cream, and stir that in too. Leave to set.

## Cinnamon Apples

1 lb. cooking apples      1 teaspoon cinnamon
2 dessertspoons sugar

Stew apples with sugar and a little water until they are tender (time depends on type of apples). Add cinnamon. Eat cold with top of the milk or cream.

## Buttered Apples (for two)

1 lb. cooking apples                    2 tablespoons sugar
piece of lemon peel (optional)    (brown if possible)
butter

Cut apples into rings, with core removed. Melt a big teaspoonful of butter and fry apple rings gently in it till tender, with the sugar sprinkled over them, and the piece of lemon peel. Turn occasionally. Eat cold, with cream if possible.

## Chocolate Mousse

For each person:

1 egg                      1 large teaspoon water
1 small nut butter    1 oz. chocolate (or a little more)

Melt chocolate with butter and water on very low flame. Separate yolk from white of each egg. Remove chocolate from heat and gradually stir in yolk. While this cools slightly, beat up whites. Mix together with fork, blending all the white but not beating it flat. Leave 12 hrs if possible.

## Chocolate Mould (for two)

1 dessertspoon each cocoa, butter, almonds (optional), sugar, broken-up biscuits
1 egg

Beat butter and cocoa. Add almonds. Dissolve sugar in a little hot water. Add to butter mixture. Beat egg lightly and add. Either grease a bowl, fill it, and hope to turn out the mould when it has set, or simply eat it from the bowl.

## Lemon Chiffon (for four)

| | |
|---|---|
| 1 teaspoon unflavoured gelatine (powdered) | 2 lemons, 4 eggs |
| ¼ cup water | 1 cup sugar, pinch of salt |

Sprinkle gelatine on the water, to soften. Beat yolks; add to them half the sugar, the juice of 1 lemon, and salt. Cook in a bowl over boiling water, if possible, or over *very* gentle heat, till it thickens. Add grated rind of both lemons (if you have no grater, add juice of second lemon instead) and the gelatine. Stir till it is dissolved. Beat the egg whites stiff. Taste lemon mixture; if rather sour, add the rest (or some) of the sugar to the egg whites, and beat agan. Mix the whites carefully into lemon mixture with fork. Allow to set.

## Lemon Custard (for four)

| | |
|---|---|
| 4 eggs | 2 or 3 tablespoons sugar |
| generous half cup water | 2 lemons |

Beat eggs with sugar till light in colour and creamy. Mix juice of both lemons with water. Add gradually to egg mixture in bowl. Put bowl over boiling water in a pan. Stir till it

thickens. Pour into another bowl or glasses and leave to set.
Eat with biscuits.

### Ginger Pears (for fresh pears that are too tough to eat: for two)

| | |
|---|---|
| 1 lb. pears | 1 dessertspoon sugar (or |
| 1 heaped teaspoon ginger | more) |

Stew the peeled and cored pears with the sugar and ginger
in a little water until they are tender – maybe 15 mins.,
depends on the pears. Let them get cold and eat with top of
the milk or cream.

### Pineapple Cake (for two)

| | |
|---|---|
| 1 small tin pineapple rings | 3 slices cake (not neces- |
| marmalade | sarily fresh) |

Open tin of pineapples; slice cake and toast it. Arrange
pieces of cake alternately with pineapple rings on plate. Heat
a little of the pineapple juice with marmalade to make a
thick syrup, and pour over. Allow to set slightly.

### Fruit Cream (if you eat a lot of tinned fruit, save the extra juice for this one: for two or three)

| | |
|---|---|
| ½ tablespoon unflavoured gelatine (powdered) | ½ pint fruit juice (or make up fruit juice to ½ pint with |
| ½ carton cream or 2 table-spoons evaporated milk | water) |

Put juice in pan. Sprinkle gelatine on it. Bring towards boil,
stirring. When gelatine is completely dissolved, stop, and
pour into a bowl to set. When it is cool and very nearly set,
beat it with a fork, and beat in cream or evaporated milk.

### Fruit Snow

As above, but add fruit pulp or leftovers instead of cream.
Baby-food fruit purée does nicely. (You can also beat fruit

into cooling packet jelly or make packet jelly with less water
and empty in a tin of fruit and its juice – the fruit may sink,
but what of it.)

## Milk Jelly

Make a jelly, either from a packet or as for Fruit Cream, but
instead of all fruit juice or water use half milk, half juice.

## Coffee Jelly

Make it like Fruit Cream, using ½ pint strong sweetened
coffee instead of fruit juice. If you use a lot of sugar, use a
little less gelatine, as the sugar helps to set it.

*Magda*. As above, but with a bar of chocolate grated into
it (or flaked with a knife) while it is hot.

## Coffee Chiffon (for two)

6 dessertspoons sugar
½ pint strong coffee, with a
little milk in it
1 dessertspoon gelatine
(powdered)

1 egg (2 if you can spare
them)
½ cup water

Dissolve gelatine in the water. Add half the sugar, and all the
coffee and milk. Beat egg yolk with other half of sugar in a
bowl over a pan of boiling water, until it thickens, stirring
constantly. Add coffee mixture, and fold in 1 or 2 beaten
egg whites.

## Coffee Cream (for two)

1 teaspoon unflavoured gelatine
(powdered)
1 dessertspoon sugar
2 eggs

4 teaspoons Nescafé
1 cup water
2 tablespoons milk or
cream

Dissolve gelatine in a little warm water. Beat eggs lightly.
Add milk and sugar. Stir in a bowl over a pan of boiling
water, until it thickens. Add gelatine, and Nescafé dissolved
in the rest of the water. Leave to set.

COOKING TO STAY ALIVE

## Summer Pudding (dead easy: for two or three)

For fresh blackcurrants, redcurrants, raspberries, black-berries, etc., or their bottled equivalents.

1 lb. soft fruit (fresh or bottled)      slices of not too fresh
sugar (if fresh fruit is used)            bread (or cake)

If fruit is fresh, stew with a little water and enough sugar to sweeten until it is soft. Cut crusts off bread and line a bowl with thin slices so that they fit closely. Put in fruit. Lay bread on top (so that fruit is completely contained), pour over any extra juice. Put a plate with a weight on it over the bread and leave 24 hrs.

## Rhubarb

The trouble with people who grow rhubarb is that they never know when to stop. If you, too, are apt to come back from a week-end in the country with enough rhubarb to feed the whole neighbourhood for a month, here are one or two ways of eating it apart from just stewed, stewed, stewed (see page 42).

## Rhubarb Cream

1 dessertspoon cornflour to each      rhubarb, sugar
  cup of stewed rhubarb

Stew the rhubarb with sugar to taste and a little water until soft and mushy. Take 1 dessertspoon cornflour to each cup of rhubarb and mix with a little cold water. Add to rhubarb and boil 5 mins. Turn into a bowl and eat when it is cold.

## Rhubarb Sponge

See Apple Cream Sponge page, 120

## Rhubarb Fool

Mix a cupful of stewed rhubarb with half a cup real custard, as on page 121.

## Rhubarb Jelly

Mix stewed rhubarb with a cooling raspberry packet jelly (as on page 124).

## Fruit Salad

It seems too simple to mention, but there is a great difference between a good fruit salad and the dismal mixtures of sour apple and sloshy orange juice that so often pose as 'fresh fruit salad' in restaurants.

1. Have at least one *interesting* fruit in predominance – even if it has to be out of a tin or frozen.
2. Carefully cut up the fresh fruit that goes in – no orange pith, no grape pips.
3. Be careful with the syrup. Do not use just the stuff from the tins, but if you can possibly manage it pack the fruit down with some sugar a few hours beforehand.

## Trifle

Good trifles are expensive; cheap ones are usually foul. Here is one that can really be a star performance and serves six.

| | |
|---|---|
| 1 packet sponge fingers or some sponge cake | 1 packet lemon-pie filling |
| 1 tin *or* frozen packet raspberries or strawberries | 1 small bottle maraschino cherries |
| ½ packet jelly, dissolved in water as directed on packet | 1 bottle double cream walnuts |
| 1 wineglass sherry or rum | 2 bananas |

First put the sponge in the bottom of a big bowl, and pour half the alcohol over it. Then melt the jelly, add about one quarter of the fruit to it, and pour over the sponge cakes. Leave that in a cool place while you make up the lemon-pie filling, according to directions on packet. When it is ready, spread half the cherries and all of the remaining fruit on to the sponge-and-jelly mixture. Pour over the rest of the alcohol, and then the lemon filling. Slice the bananas and add to the filling. Some will sink in, some won't. Near the time of serving, whip the cream, add a heaped teaspoon of sugar to it, spread evenly on trifle and – at the last moment, because they sometimes sink in – decorate with the remaining cherries and the halved walnuts.

Whatever else you leave out, don't leave out the fruit.

*Five oddments that your friends can eat with their fingers*

## Mendiant Espagnol

For each person:

a handful of mixed sweet nuts and raisins, 2–4 large dried figs

Stuff each fig with the mixture of crushed nuts and raisins, until they are plump to bursting point. Hand round on a big plate.

## Charoseth

For each person:

half an eating apple              1 heaped teaspoon sultanas
a few chopped almonds          pinch of cinnamon

Chop the apple very finely indeed (grate if possible), mix with the other things, and press into little balls. Dust with sugar. (You could use some of the fruit and nuts left over from the last recipe.)

## Coffee Balls (strictly for porridge eaters)

1 cup porridge oats                        1 teaspoon sugar
1 tablespoon or more strong coffee    a nut of butter
1 heaped teaspoon cocoa

Beat butter to a cream; stir in cocoa mixed with oats, and coffee, alternately. Shape it into balls. Dust in caster sugar.

## Nut Brittle

2 cups sugar     $\frac{1}{4}$ lb. roasted almonds

Melt the sugar over very gentle heat, stirring all the time, till it is a syrup. Drop in almonds. Stir till well coated. Drop out in little clumps on a plate. Do not offer to people with shaky teeth.

## Chocolate Munch

1 4-oz. bar chocolate or more     1 cup cornflakes or less

Melt chocolate in a very little water. Drop in cornflakes. Form into balls. Allow to set.

✳✳✳✳✳✳✳✳✳✳✳✳✳✳✳✳✳✳✳✳✳✳✳✳✳

## CHAPTER 9
# Coffee and Tea

### Coffee

WHAT sort of coffee you buy depends, obviously, on what
sort you like. If you like pure, mild coffee, it will be more
expensive than French black after-dinner coffee, both because chicory is often added to the latter and because its
method of roasting helps to disguise the flavour of slightly
poorer quality coffees. Buy your coffee in small quantities,
so that it is fresh. It comes no more expensive this way.

If you have a percolator, an espresso machine, a filter jug,
or a Cona, there is no difficulty – simply follow the directions
given by the maker, or the advice of the person who had it
last. And keep it CLEAN – it makes a fantastic difference to
the taste. If you have no machine, it is almost essential to
have a strainer – it only costs about sixpence – and even then
it is as well to leave the strained coffee by the fire for five
minutes, and to put a tablespoon of cold water into it (without stirring), to help the fine grit settle to the bottom.

1. *Jug method.* Make as for tea. Pour boiling water on to
grounds, in the proportion of one heaped dessertspoon per
small cup; stir once or twice; leave for a minute or two;
strain; stand to settle.

2. *Pan method.* Use same proportions of coffee. Sprinkle it
on the heating water and let it come nearly to the boil BUT
NOT QUITE. Keep it just under boiling point until it is as
dark as you want it; strain, stand near fire to settle. If it is
impossible to strain it because you have no other bowl or pot,
let it stand anyway, and then strain it into the cup without
re-stirring.

Incidentally, there is one powerful smell closely associated with the making of coffee in bedsitters which has nothing to do with coffee at all – as I discovered once by forgetting to put any grounds in the pot. It is the smell of burning plastic, and will go away if you move the handle of the pot away from the flame.

If you like hot milk with your coffee, heat some milk – but *boiled* milk has an unpleasant flavour all its own and is usually bad for the surrounding carpet.

## Iced Coffee

You may think this is impossible without a refrigerator, but actually the creamy German sort can be made very well, if you have the time.

Make some strong coffee and add sugar – rather more than usual – while it is still hot. Let it stand until absolutely cold – overnight if possible. Then pour into big glasses and put a lump of ice cream – about half a normal small brick – on top of each one, and stir a little of it in.

## Tea

Everybody knows how to make tea – but it may not have occurred to everyone that a kettle and a teapot are not essentials. A saucepan to boil the water, and a jug with a saucer on it, will do very well.

Or there are always TEABAGS. Our resolute national refusal to tolerate anything but Real Tea in a Pot is generally held to show our moral superiority to the Americans; and it is certainly true that teabags cannot be spoken of in the same breath as Lapsang Suchong prayerfully infused in a porcelain Wedgwood pot – preferably by a Duchess in a tea-gown. But if the alternative would be the cheapest possible Indian, brewed till you can stand the spoon up in it, and just as good with condensed milk as without, you have nothing to lose with teabags except face. It is so much easier to use a teabag, if you only want one cup; and you avoid all that sordid wearisome business of emptying the pot. Unless you like it really *black*, it is better to dip the teabag up and down several times than to leave it stewing in the tea.

You could always compromise with one of those spoons with holes in that holds the tea leaves together while you dip it in a cup. (Called an infuser.)

I remember crossing into Canada from the States with another British exile, and with tears in our eyes ordering tea in a real pot. It came, and we drank it with cries of loyal rapture – only to find when we complimented the waitress that there was a teabag *in the pot*.

***********************************

CHAPTER 10

# Two Rings

A GOOD many bedsitters are equipped with a sort of double gas ring, which offers rather more scope to the cook than a single ring. A really expert cook can do almost anything with two burners except bake; but for most of us the chief advantage is that the time of cooking can be cut down by cooking vegetables and main dishes simultaneously. Most of the recipes already given that require potatoes or rice cooked beforehand can be speeded up by cooking the starchy food alongside the rest of it – spaghetti, for instance, or sausages and mash, or saucepan fish pie. With others, you can boil the potatoes separately instead of frying them alongside the meat, or you can pad out a rather less filling dish by adding potatoes to it. Remember that there's nothing to stop you boiling two vegetables together – potatoes and carrots, rice and onion.

The recipes that follow are no more than a few suggestions for you to work on. For really inexperienced two-ring cooks, it is worth while blowing two shillings on an admirable Ministry of Food pamphlet called *The ABC of Cookery*, which assumes you know nothing *at all* and practically starts by drawing a picture of an egg and saying 'This is an Egg'.

One of the chief advantages of two-ring cooking is that it enables you to use a method of cooking rice which is absolutely foolproof in all circumstances.

## Rice

First put on a kettle, with a little water in it. Then put a spoonful of fat into your heaviest saucepan. When it is hot, turn some measured rice in it for just a minute or two, until

133

it is transparent; then add exactly twice as much very hot water as you had rice. Add salt, pepper, a bay leaf if you have or like it. Clamp the lid on, with a cloth between the lid and pan. Put on asbestos, on lowest possible gas, for exactly half an hour.

At the end it will be dry and fluffy and ready to eat. It can stand for up to ten minutes without getting cold.

The advantage of this method is that, having got the rice on, you don't give it another thought until you want to eat it, thus leaving your mind and hands free to make whatever else you are eating.

## MAIN DISHES WHICH NEED A SEPARATE VEGETABLE

### Devilled Drumsticks (two helpings)

| | |
|---|---|
| 1 small packet frozen chicken drumsticks | 1 chicken soup cube |
| | ¼ teaspoon mustard |
| 1 dessertspoon Worcester sauce | salt, pepper |
| 1 dessertspoon flour | 1 teaspoon butter |

Make a sauce with butter, the flour, and a half pint of water in which the soup cube has been dissolved. (White sauce method, page 42.) Add everything else, and simmer for 20 mins. Serve with rice. (½ hr.)

### Fricadeller

| | |
|---|---|
| ¼ lb. pork mince | 1 egg |
| 1 small dessertspoon flour | salt, pepper, a little milk |

Mix all together and form into rissoles. Fry, in deep fat if possible; and eat with spinach. (10 mins.)

### Chicken Maryland (two helpings)

| | |
|---|---|
| 1 packet frozen chicken | 1 small packet or tin sweetcorn |
| 1 banana | |
| 2 oz. mushrooms (optional) | breadcrumbs |
| butter | 1 egg |

134

Beat egg lightly on plate; dip chicken pieces first in egg, then in breadcrumbs. Fry on medium heat for 15 mins., turning occasionally; then add the banana (sliced in two lengthways) and the mushrooms, lower the gas slightly and simmer another 7–10 mins. Cook the sweetcorn in a small pan on the other ring. At the last minute drain it and add a good lump of butter. (30 mins.)

## Creole Liver

1 pimento (sweet pepper)  
garlic, salt, pepper, parsley (optional)

¼ lb. liver, 2 tomatoes  
oil, pinch of chilli powder

Start to cook rice, perhaps by the method described at the beginning of this chapter. When it is under way, put a spoonful of olive oil into the frying pan. Add the chopped liver, chopped pimento, and pinch of chilli, a chopped clove of garlic, salt, pepper, and after a few minutes a spoonful of water and the seasonings. Stir, and cook gently for 5 mins. or a little longer. Put on to a plate, and sit it on top of the cooking rice to keep warm. Add another spoonful of oil to the pan, and a couple of chopped tomatoes. Cook gently 5–7 mins. Heap rice, liver, and tomatoes separately on your plate. (20–35 mins. depending on how you cook the rice.)

## Pork Chops with Red Cabbage

1 or 2 pork chops  
salt, pepper, parsley, and/or herbs

half a red cabbage  
1 dessertspoon flour  
lemon juice

Cook pork chops 3 mins. each side in hot fat, reduce gas, and cook more gently another 20 mins. Meanwhile boil cabbage in salted water for 30 mins. Drain cabbage, keeping the liquid. Remove chops from pan. Put flour into the fat, mix thoroughly, gradually add cabbage water and seasonings. Put the chops back into the sauce to reheat, and the cabbage into its own pan over low gas, for a few seconds. (40 mins.)

## Creamed Shrimps

1 teaspoon butter, dessert-
    spoon flour, cup milk
salt, pepper, parsley

1 small packet shrimps
anchovy essence (optional)

Make white sauce, as on page 42. Simmer 5 mins. Add
seasoning, anchovy essence, and shrimps and simmer another 5–10 mins. Eat with green peas, fresh or frozen for
choice; or with mashed potatoes. (20 mins.)

## Mushroom Patties

1 onion
1 tablespoon breadcrumbs or
    crumbled bread
salt, pepper, parsley (optional)

2 oz. mushrooms
1 egg
3 dessertspoons flour

Mix yolk and flour and enough water to make a thick dough
that does not stick to the fingers. Beat egg-white stiff, and
fold in.

Meanwhile chop up mushrooms and fry with onion until
all is tender. Add breadcrumbs. Cut dough (rolled out with
a bottle) into 2-in. squares, put some of the mushroom
mixture on each, fold across triangularly, and drop into
boiling water. Boil 5 mins. Serve with a green vegetable
rather than with potatoes. (20 mins.)

## Pigeon (a pigeon is just right for one hungry person)

1 pigeon
1 dessertspoon flour
1 onion

1 rasher
salt, pepper, herbs, fat

Fry rasher and onions 5 mins. Put in pigeon, chopped in two
– get the man you buy it from to do it for you – and turn it
in fat on all sides. Mix in flour, carefully; add 3 tablespoons
water and seasonings. Simmer 20 mins. or longer if pigeon
is old. (40 mins.)

## *Rabbit with Prunes* (two helpings)

4 bits of cut-up rabbit
1 small tin prunes *or* ¼ lb. soaked dried prunes

vinegar
herbs, bay leaf, salt, pepper
1 dessertspoon flour

If possible soak the rabbit in vinegar overnight – which would give you time to soak the prunes in water too. Pour off vinegar, and sprinkle the rabbit chunks with flour. Turn them in hot fat until they are browned on all sides. Add prunes, flavouring, and enough of the prune juice just to cover. Simmer for 1 hr. Mashed potatoes or a green vegetable with this. (1 hr 10 mins.)

## *Veal Parmesan*

1 veal cutlet or escalope
olive oil, salt, pepper

2 dessertspoons grated cheese

Cut off white bits (and, if you like, bone) from cutlet; beat it out flat and press grated cheese on both sides. Cook in hot olive oil – about 3 mins. each side. (10 mins.)

## *Braised Beefsteak or Pork Chops in Cider*

¼lb. braising steak *or* 1 large pork chop
oil

garlic, bay leaf, herbs, pepper
2 tablespoons *dry* cider

Fry steak or chop (beaten if steak) for about 2 mins. each side over medium flame. Add herbs and seasonings and the cider (and some half cooked potatoes, if you like). Put the lid on, and cook as slowly as possible for an hour. (1 hr 10 mins.)

## *Meat Balls in Tomato Sauce*

1 tablespoon sausage meat
  1 tablespoon minced beef
  (*or* 2 tablespoons of either)
1 small tin tomatoes

1 egg
1 onion
fat

Mix egg, finely chopped onion, and meat together, with salt and pepper. Shape into balls. Fry 5 mins. so that all sides are browned. Empty tin of tomatoes over this. Stir and cook gently 10–15 mins. depending on how large you have made the meat balls – the smaller the quicker. (20–25 mins.)

## VEGETABLES

The times for cooking standard vegetables in boiling water are given in the Beginner's Index.

### Braised Celery

One head of celery is ample for one, possible for two. Cut off the hard hub at the bottom and the feathery leaves at the top. Boil 10 mins. in salted water. Drain, shake, and finish cooking slowly in butter, with the lid on if possible. (20 mins.)

### Braised Chicory (for those who like its acrid flavour; those who don't, see page 31)

Cut off hard hub, but otherwise leave each head alone. Allow one per person. Cook slowly in butter until tender – about 20 mins. At the last minute add salt and a squeeze of lemon juice. (20–30 mins.)

### Cabbage Caraway

Cook cabbage in a very little boiling salted water in the ordinary way, but with a few caraway seeds thrown in; and when it is done (but not soggy) drain off the water and add 2 dessertspoons per half cabbage of sour milk or yoghourt. (15 mins.)

### Cooked Cucumbers

Half cucumber per person. Peel it and cut it into chunks. Cook in a very little water with mint, salt and pepper, with the lid on. If you feel up to making a white sauce (see page 42) to cover the cucumber, that makes it nicer still. (15 mins.)

## Harvard Beets

Buy cooked beetroots, one small one per person. Peel. Heat
gently with a little oil in covered pan. Make a white sauce
(see page 42) and add 1 dessertspoon vinegar, 1 teaspoon
sugar (for 2).

## Cabbage (a more interesting way than just boiled)

Half small cabbage                1 onion
oil for frying                    garlic, salt, pepper

Fry onion and garlic in a very little oil 5 mins. Add chopped
cabbage, salt, pepper, and 3 tablespoons water. Simmer very
gently 20 mins., taking care it does not burn. (25 mins.)

## Tomatoes Provençale

Strictly speaking, these should be grilled; but even fried
halved tomatoes can be given this special taste, if you rub the
cut face with garlic, sprinkle each with herbs, salt, and
pepper, and put a drop or two of olive oil on each. Let them
stand for a while beforehand, if you are going to fry them.

## Aubergine and Yoghourt

1 aubergine                       2 dessertspoons yoghourt
olive oil                         salt

Slice the aubergine lengthways, dust with salt, and leave for
15 mins. Wipe off the dew that will have formed, and fry the
slices in olive oil till soft – about 10 mins. At the last moment,
dollop the yoghourt into the pan. (25 mins.)

## Red Cabbage

half a red cabbage                1 onion
1 apple                           vinegar, sugar, oil

Slice apple, onion, and cabbage. Heat fat in pan with a lid.
Add vegetables and sugar. Pour over vinegar. Simmer ½ hr.
(35 mins.)

## PART TWO

# COOKING TO IMPRESS

*********************************

## CHAPTER 11

# Problems and Answers

IMPRESSING visitors can usually be done in two ways: the Lavish and the Casual. For you in your bedsitter the lavish is impossible. You cannot put on a show of Crown Derby, snow-white linen, and gleaming silver any more than you can produce a sucking-pig with an orange in its mouth; and any attempts at grandeur will merely look pathetic. So instead you must concentrate on the apparently effortless meal – the attitude of 'just a little thing I seem to have cooking in this pot'. But there you are, you and your gas ring, right in the room with your visitors: there can be no slamming the kitchen door on a cloud of black smoke and coming forward with a gay, brave smile. Yet it is vital not to look flustered; for although in fact it is harder to produce a decent meal on a gas ring than in a kitchen, the impression you will give if things go wrong is of not *even* being able to produce a simple gas ring meal without fuss.

If your guests are not to see you looking flustered over your cooking, this in practice means that they had better not see you cooking at all. Heroines in novels may be 'discovered' poised gracefully over a rather advanced sauce; in real life a girl is more apt to be red in the face and stirring furiously at the lumps. So the first rule for producing good dinners in bedsitters is: *Get as much as you possibly can done beforehand*. I would say it was almost essential to be in the evening before. (If your bedsitter is anything like any bedsitter I've ever lived in, it will need cleaning up anyway.) Make a casserole, and a cold pudding that can set over night, and then all you will have to do the next day is prepare any salad or first course you are having, heat up the casserole, and lay out the knives and forks.

I do realize that this is not always possible, so I have given recipes for preparing the same day as well.

Whether you are doing most of the work the day before or not, there is another rule that most hostesses follow if they want peace of mind, bedsitters or no: *Never have more than one thing that needs last-minute attention.* If you have decided to cook a delicious Zabaione for your guests, have something cold with mayonnaise and a crisp salad beforehand. If you are doing some aromatic Italian veal thing that needs a little praying over at the last minute, make sure that everything else is absolutely ready before you start.

The third rule concerns the sad fact that no one is ever going to be impressed by anything that comes out of a tin, a bottle, or a packet – if they know that it has done so. Fortunately those who sneer at tinned food outnumber those who can actually detect its presence by about ten to one, so you can use what tins you like in the cooking, provided you can *get rid of the evidence* in time – though there's no denying that on the whole, the more fresh food there is in your dishes the better they will taste, and it takes a very skilled cook indeed to make something really delectable out of all-prepacked food.

If in normal life you rely heavily on teabags, Nescafé, sliced super-bread, bottled ketchup and mayonnaise, and evaporated milk, stick them into a suitcase under the bed well before your guests arrive – or leave them with a neighbour, if you can be sure of getting them back. You can always get away with a simple meal, if all the details are right – really fresh, crisp, crusty bread (*not* blotting-paper in plastic packets), good butter and not old marg, fresh and real coffee, and real cream if you are having cream (the most indifferent puddings become eatable with enough cream), and really good cheeses. It is far better to spend money on getting these things perfect than on trying to cram in another course or putting three more ingredients in the salad.

Then there is the problem illustrated by this quotation from *The Dud Avocado*:

'Any moron can cook a steak,' I kept saying to myself, as I went about my work in the kitchen early Thursday evening. I was not only going to give them something to get their teeth into, but I was going to serve it to them all by myself.

Everybody was terribly kind and cooperative at dinner, and it took all four of us ceaselessly moiling and toiling from kitchen to studio and back again to organize and consume a simple meal of soup, steak and onions, peas and potatoes, and salad. And even then the process was simplified by my just leaving the loaf of bread, just simply forgetting it and leaving it at the bottom of the shopping-bag.

Exactly. The 'complicated' casserole is child's play compared to the simple steak. *Don't serve too many bits.* Don't, if it comes to that, try to stuff your guests too full – only one heavy course, *please*. And remember that there is no possible polite answer to the questions, 'Oh, I forgot the mushrooms – would you have liked some?'

If you cannot prepare it all beforehand, and have to do it after you come home from work, follow this order of procedure.

1. Finish any cleaning. You can finish cooking without shame in front of your visitors, but you cannot very well sweep under their embarrassed feet.

2. Set the table – it will reassure people that they have come on the right day, and that there *will* be a meal eventually.

3. Get yourself looking nice. In a house you can disappear and finish dressing – in a bedsitter, no. Besides, you want your friends to think that dark-eyed look is all Soul, not just mascara; and they won't, if they see you putting it on.

4. And now get on with the cooking, throwing out the papers and cans as fast as possible as you go.

One final point: it is better to serve a simple meal for which you have enough knives and forks and plates, than something elaborate which requires that you spend five minutes clattering on the landing between courses, washing up. Be French about this: make people use the same knives and forks, propped up on a bit of bread.

*Some ways round the plate-and-cutlery shortage*

1. Serve as a first course one of the dishes listed on pages 108–10, all of which can be eaten in the fingers and served off a single big plate.

2. Cut up a French loaf and butter it just before your guests arrive. (You can keep it fresh, wrapped in a *slightly* damp cloth, if you want to do it a little beforehand.) That way, they help themselves from a single plate or basket, and need no bread plates and bread knives.

3. Dish up puddings in glasses if you happen to have more glasses than plates.

4. Eat light, fluffy puddings with teaspoons, if you have more teaspoons than dessertspoons. Makes it go further, anyway.

5. A hot snack – rolls toasted at the fire stuffed with hamburger, or devilled chicken, hot dogs, toast rarebit, etc. – can be handed round in paper table napkins (which is, incidentally, about the only time paper napkins are socially OK. If you care).

6. Scallop shells come free with scallops. So it is worth having scallops once or twice, to equip yourself with these excellent dishes for fishy first courses.

7. If your friends like Coke (count me out), Coke bottles and straws are easier than glasses – but don't drink beer through straws.

## WHO ARE YOU TRYING TO IMPRESS?

All the foregoing remarks apply whoever your guests may be. For subtler effects, it is worth studying your particular type of visitor; and they come, as far as I can see, into four categories. (I am not counting parties, which are dealt with in the Drinks chapter.)

1. The troglodyte in the next bedsitter.

2. Couples, or mixed singles, who are accustomed to kitchen food and drawing-room standards. They have forgotten what it was like to cook in a bedsitter (if they ever knew), and it is your business not to remind them.

3. Your parents, or your parents' spies – who are there to reassure themselves that you are eating adequately, get to bed early, know no vicious young men, and breathe plenty of clean fresh air.

4. Delicious little parties à deux.

For the troglodyte, it is hardly necessary to embark on this section at all, except by way of practice; just eat your way gently through Part One and be thankful for an undemanding friend.

Impressing the couples is hardest of all, since you must be a host or hostess in the ordinary way as well as cook, and since their standards will be the highest. For them, I should say it was essential to prepare things the evening before; and for them two standard rules become vital: DON'T FUSS, and DON'T APOLOGIZE. Above all you must avoid an air of diffidence, of deferring to their superior experience. You just take it for granted that *of course* civilized people have high standards of food, and that is all there is to it. Avoid the consciously chi-chi in decoration – no, absolutely *no* candles in bottles; and be sure there is enough to drink.

The key to entertaining the folks back home is to lay emphasis on neatness and foods that are wholesome and don't smell; and to avoid trying to impress them (as you would certainly try to impress anyone else) with your knowledge of un-English cooking. For their benefit, I have included one or two things like Lancashire Hot-pot; and if you are ever going to make a steamed pudding, now is the time (use a mix or a tin); and don't waste money on buying them drink, which will only make them uneasy about how much you normally stash away. Sit this lot at a table, however many jars of face-cream and unfinished masterpieces you have to sweep off it first; and borrow a tablecloth if you can.

It is impossible to discuss parties *à deux* without addressing the he's and the she's separately. Let us first consider:

## COOKING FOR A MAN

Elementary rules: avoid all whimsy and complication in the food. Don't have elaborate little salad dishes to start with, or end up with too sweet a last course. Cheese – good cheese, and plenty of it – is better. Drink is essential here; and better good beer than grocer's sherry or Babycham. (See Chapter 15.) You may allow him to make himself at home by wielding a corkscrew and making the toast, but nothing else. His zeal to help you wash up will be quenched like a candle in a storm when he actually sees that sink.

It does no harm to imply, very subtly, that your standards of food are just a little higher than his – but be careful, if in fact he is an international gourmet and you opened your first can of Grade B ravioli only a fortnight back. Don't apologize much if anything goes wrong; don't flap, whatever happens; and NEVER ask 'Is it all right?'

There is one class of man for whom a quite different routine is needed: the richie who has up till now bought you expensive meals in smart places – often your only decent meal that week – and now, to your horror, wants to get to know you better in your own surroundings. You don't want him to think that you can't be bothered to cook for him, or can't stand him around the place, or else he will naturally never ask you out again. But equally, neither the food nor the atmosphere must be so inviting that he decides to give up eating out altogether in favour of eating in. The dodge here is to reverse the normal procedure, and fuss up and down constantly; make it clear that you are trying desperately to please, but make sure that ten minutes do not go by without your rushing to your feet to make this or remove that or see to the other; and have a few people dropping in throughout the evening. He will quickly conclude that your own surroundings hold little promise for him, and go back to taking you to Boulestin's, or of course luring you back to his own lush flat. Well, at least he has to see to the food there.

## COOKING FOR A GIRL

You, as a man, can get away with more roughness than a girl can. But if you are seriously luring the girl, you have a dilemma: you certainly don't want to give her the idea that you are struggling to impress her, but of course she will be touched and appreciative of any sign that shows you have remembered who it is you are feeding. The right compromise is to imply that you set *yourself* rather high standards of food; but add, almost as an afterthought, something of purely feminine appeal, like sticky chocolates or her own special brand of Turkish cigarettes. (Incidentally, there is no reason to suppose that the better you cook for her, the better she will cook for you on the return match. If she thinks you are a second Escoffier, she may just get terribly flustered.)

Do not, at any time, invite a girl to dinner, and when she arrives in a pretty frock, looking forward to a drink and a little cossetting, present her with several odd-looking tins, packets, and lumps and expect *her* to do the cooking. If she knows her onions, she will immediately make one of the following remarks:

1. 'Oh darling, I'm so tired – just make me some coffee and never mind about the food.'

2. 'Oh darling, I'm so tired – let's go out instead. I know a lovely little restaurant up the hill, and it's not *really* expensive.'

3. 'Honey, I've been cooking for other people all week [i.e. not for you, you clot]. I just couldn't face it. *You* do it.'

Even if you bludgeon her into doing the work, she will do it grudgingly and without noticeable skill.

*Asking* a girl to come and cook for you is quite another matter – and we are all gullible enough to take it as a compliment. Watch out, however, that she does not take it as

a sign for turning up with an outsize apron, five saucepans,
and a matrimonial gleam in her eye.

DO NOT ASK HER TO WASH UP.

## THE THIRD PAW

Every dog has four thoughts, one for each paw: food, food,
sex, and food. Most of this book is naturally concerned with
preoccupations 1, 2, and 4; but the other thought also has its
own special problems in a bedsitter.

The chief trouble, for man or girl, is that everything in a
bedsitter is so *visible*. Unless you work it all out with greatest
care, your visitor can see at a glance just exactly what you
expect or hope for or hope to avoid. However, there are two
saving facts: men can count on a girl never really knowing
how much drink a man would be likely to keep for his own
consumption; and a girl can reckon that unless she makes a
great display of falling over herself to prepare things, no man
will ever realize quite how much trouble has gone into a meal.
One of the most carefully-prepared meals of my life provoked
several appreciative remarks from the man in question about
'those unplanned, carefree, golden days that sometimes just
*happen*'. Ha!

If one of you has asked the other to dinner, it is reasonable
to suppose that a certain amount of preparation will have
gone towards it; and so long as you do nothing as crude as
putting a red sock over the light bulb to give it a romantic
glow, or (conversely) jamming the door so that it won't quite
shut, you only have to apply the general rules for entertaining, modify them slightly as suggested above, and you will
do all right.

The casual invitation, whoever gives it, is rather more
tricky – especially if it isn't really casual at all. Here again, I
feel obliged to address you separately.

## ASKING HIM UP

The problem here is to make sure that everything is looking nice without anything looking planned. (Let us hope he does not realize that the room only ever *does* look neat when there is company expected.) Soup in a thermos and stuffed rolls for two is a little too deliberate; but you can always pretend that some delicious thing in a saucepan is left over from the day before, or dig in your food box as if you had no idea what was there and you just often do have a tin of *foie gras* handy.

If you are not sure of the state of the room, *don't ask him in*. Many is the young man I have horrified by saying, 'Oh, do come in, I'll have it all cleared up in a minute', picking the dirty clothes out of the fender as I spoke. For dissuading him, you cannot, of course, use the old gag of 'My great-aunt sleeps so lightly'; and it is unwise to say the landlady allows no men visitors, if there's any chance that she (or you) will have changed her mind another time. Two possible blocks are, 'I'm afraid I've lent my room to the girl next door for the evening – she's got friends in. You must come to dinner some other night and see my hovel' or 'I won't ask you up tonight – the gas-fire is broken and it's all a bit bleak' (following this up with a stern refusal to put him to the bother of coming up and fixing it for you).

Do not, whatever you do, tell him the truth and say: 'You can't come up, because I haven't made the bed.'

## ASKING HER UP

Your big snag is that *either* the room will be chilly and un-inviting enough to dispel all the warm *camaraderie* of the evening so far, *or* it will be only too clear that the impromptu invitation was in fact part of a deep-laid plot. Having the gas-fire on is as clear a pointer to your intentions as a champagne bottle cooling under the tap. One way round this is to burst into the room with the words, 'Dammit, I left the gas-fire on again.' But I know one man who says that he once did this only to find that the fire had been out for hours – no shillings in the meter.

If you have a set of rough and ready house rules designed to protect the amorous from casual interruptions, DON'T put these precautions into force unless you really mean business. Nothing causes the timid fawn to shy away faster than the feeling that the rest of the house knows what she is in for (especially if she hopes she isn't). A towel hung over the outside door handle may lose you game, set, and match.

## ✳✳✳✳✳✳✳✳✳✳✳✳✳✳✳✳✳✳✳✳✳✳✳✳✳

CHAPTER 12

# Suggestions for the First Course

THE following dishes make good first courses for when you
have people to dinner. Any of the cold dishes listed on
page 108–10 would also be suitable.

MELON: Serve sugar with it, and ginger if possible. Divide
into good big slices and scrape out seeds. It is not worth
paying a fortune for an out-of-season melon – it will have
no flavour anyway.

GRAPEFRUIT: Prepare it some time before, by cutting all
the way round each half, cutting along each section, and
removing the white bit from the centre. Sprinkle with
sugar, and leave it to soak up.

AVOCADO PEAR: See Salad section.

SALADE NIÇOISE: See Salad section.

PRAWN COCKTAIL: Prepare in glasses. Put some shredded
lettuce in the bottom of each glass. Mix prawns with this
dressing: 1 carton single cream, salt, pepper, a squeeze of
tomato paste or a dash of ketchup. (Cayenne pepper or
Worcester sauce are nice too, but not essential.)

POTTED SHRIMPS: Buy them ready potted. Hand round
fresh, thin brown bread and butter.

SAITHE: Rather like smoked salmon (but don't try to
pretend it *is*). Serve with, or on, brown bread and butter,
with lemon juice.

SOUP: If you serve a tinned or packet soup, do something
to it to make it look more like your own work. (See Soup
chapter.) A jug by the fire, or a thermos, is a help here.

HORS D'ŒUVRE: Buy a few nice oddments at a delicatessen – rollmops, or black olives, or Italian salad – and
make into an hors d'œuvre by adding radishes, or tomatoes,
or halved hard-boiled eggs.

PÂTÉ: Buy it in little red tins, or fresh from a delicatessen. Serve with fresh toast (which your guests can help make).

CORN ON THE COB: See page 70. You need paper napkins for this, and your guests will get into a complete mess, but it may help to break the ice, and anyway you need no knives and forks. (Casserole can heat up before you cook the corn, go back on while you are eating it.)

BUTTERED CRAB: See page 99.

DEVILLED HERRING ROES: See page 96. A nice cheap one; as with Corn on the Cob, start the reheating of the main dish before you put the roes on to cook.

STUFFED TOMATOES or STUFFED PIMENTOES: See page 64. Cooked beforehand and reheated. *Warning:* they are filling, so have a less filling second course. And of course allow less per person than you would if they were to be the main course.

GNOCCHI: See page 76. Make up the mixture into little balls and get rid of the mess before your guests arrive. (This is a good filling first course, but don't do it for company until you have practised for yourself.)

RAVIOLI: See page 76. Another filling opener. You could also, if entertaining only one honoured guest, buy frozen ravioli and heat it gently, as it is very good. (But it is very expensive, so uneconomic for a larger number.)

CHICKEN LIVERS ON TOAST: See page 58. If there's plenty of toast and not too much chicken liver, you could just about manage without knives and forks.

CHEESE FONDUE: See page 113.

**\*\*\*\*\*\*\*\*\*\*\*\*\*\*\*\*\*\*\*\*\*\*\*\***

## CHAPTER 13

# Main-Course Dishes

## TO BE MADE THE PREVIOUS DAY

### Poulet Marengo (for four)

1 large chunk of chicken per person (*or* 1 good-sized chicken for four, cut up)
1 teaspoon tomato paste
herbs, bay leaf, salt, pepper

2 or 3 onions (optional)
6 tomatoes
¼ lb. mushrooms
olive oil or butter
1 dessertspoon flour

Put a tablespoon of oil or butter in your heavy pan; turn the chicken pieces in the oil until browned on every side (and onions, if you are using them). Remove them to a plate. Stir flour into fat, and add half small cup wine, or meat extract mixed with water, or chicken bouillon and water – or just water. Mix. Add flavourings, mushrooms washed and chopped, and pieces of chicken. Simmer on lowest possible gas for ¾ hr. Eat with rice, which you will cook before you put chicken on to warm. (1–1¼ hrs.)

NOTE You can do this one on the same day if you wish, but in that case leave out the onions, which will make your room smell.

### Chicken Mexicana (for four)

1 large chunk of chicken per person
2 pimentoes (red if possible)
1 dessertspoon flour; meat extract and water

squeeze of tomato paste
6 tomatoes
3 onions
pinch chilli powder (essential)
olive oil, salt, herbs, bay leaf

Proceed exactly as for Poulet Marengo, adding pimentoes

instead of mushrooms, and the different flavourings. (1–1$\frac{1}{4}$ hrs.)

## Chicken Paprikash (for four)

| | |
|---|---|
| 1 large chunk of chicken per person | 2 tomatoes |
| 4 medium potatoes or more | 1 pimento |
| 1 cup meat extract and water | 1 dessertspoon |
| 2 or 3 tablespoons sour cream | paprika (essen- |
| 1 large onion | tial) |

Dust the chicken pieces in flour. Fry onions in heavy saucepan till brown, add chicken pieces, and fry them till browned all over. Add everything except the sour cream, and simmer $\frac{3}{4}$ hr or longer. Next day, warm gently and add sour cream just before serving. (Needs no accompaniment.) (1$\frac{1}{4}$ hrs.)

## Chicken Pilaff (for four)

1 cupful at least pieces cooked chicken
(you can buy chickens ready cooked in big towns; or buy some pieces of chicken and boil them gently $\frac{1}{2}$ hr, keeping the liquid)

| | |
|---|---|
| 2 chicken soup cubes | herbs, bay leaf, |
| 4 onions | salt, pepper |
| handful walnuts or raisins (optional) | oil or butter |
| 1$\frac{1}{2}$ cups rice | |
| 2 tomatoes (optional) | |

First heat up water or liquid in which chicken has cooked. Fry chopped-up chicken and onion, in butter if possible, for 7 mins. Add rice and turn in fat until transparent. Add peeled tomatoes and walnuts or raisins. Then add 4 cups stock or water with soup cubes dissolved in it, and bubble merrily for 20 mins. Next day, add a little more water or stock if necessary, to heat it up, and if possible leave for 5 mins. *after* it has reheated, keeping warm but not cooking. (30 mins.)

## Danish Boiled Chicken (for four)

| | |
|---|---|
| 4 chunks chicken | 4 large potatoes |
| 1 tablespoon flour | 1 teaspoon sugar |
| 1 teaspoon or more horse-radish sauce | herbs (tarragon if possible) |
| | salt, pepper |

Put chicken in pan with potatoes, salt, pepper, herbs, and water to cover. Boil till chicken is tender – ½ hr if a roaster, 1½ hrs if a boiler (don't boil too fiercely). Leave to cool in the water.

The next day, melt a dessertspoon butter in the small saucepan, add a tablespoon of flour, stir till blended over low heat, and gradually add some of the liquid the chicken cooked in. Stir till it thickens; if too thick, add more stock; if too thin, boil hard for a few minutes. Add sugar, a big dash of horseradish sauce (out of a bottle does fine), and tarragon if you have it, more herbs if not. Cook gently five minutes, and add chicken to reheat, minus skin, bones, or anything else you feel you would be better without. Stand near fire while you cook frozen peas. (First day ½–1½ hrs, second day 20 mins.)


## Lamb Casserole (for four)

| | |
|---|---|
| 1 lb. lamb, not too fat (or 4 large lamb chops) | 1 large aubergine |
| 2 onions | 4 tomatoes, peeled |
| 1 cup rice | herbs, meat extract, salt and pepper, bay leaf |
| oil | |

Remove fat and bone from lamb, and fry quickly on all sides in olive oil in heavy saucepan, with chopped onions and the aubergine (cut into chunks but not peeled). Fry a few minutes. Add rice and turn till transparent. Add seasonings, and 1 cup water with meat extract dissolved in it. Simmer on lowest possible heat 1½ hrs or more, adding more water if it begins to dry up. Wine, either red or white, can be used instead of part of the stock to very good effect. (2 hrs.)

## Greek Lamb Casserole (for four)

| | |
|---|---|
| 1 lb. lamb (or 4 large lamb chops) | 6–8 tomatoes |
| ½ teaspoon rosemary or mixed herbs | garlic, salt, pepper, |
| 6 potatoes | olive oil |

Divide the meat into pieces such that each person will get two or three, put a sliver of garlic into the flesh of each one (or if you are using lamb chops, keep whole and put garlic between meat and bone). Brown them in olive oil. Add peeled tomatoes, sliced potatoes, herbs, salt, and pepper. Cook as slowly as possible for as long as possible. Add more water if it needs it, but if you keep the heat down it shouldn't. (1½–2½ hrs.)

## Lancashire Hot-pot (for four)

| | |
|---|---|
| 1 lb. cheap mutton | 4–6 potatoes |
| 2 onions | ¼ lb. mushroom stalks |
| 2 oz. mushrooms | 1 kidney |

Halve mushrooms, chop stalks. Cut excess fat from mutton; cut into chunks. Slice onion thinly. Remove white core from kidney, and cut into chunks. Brown mutton in butter; add salt and pepper and enough water to come half-way up the pan. Simmer for at least 1½ hours, adding kidney 15 mins. from the end. You can zizz this up with a cup of red wine, herbs, bay leaf, and even garlic – but then it is not authentic Lancashire, of course. (2 hrs.)

## Lamb Pilaff (makes four helpings cheaply, so worth the apparent bother)

| | |
|---|---|
| 4 small lamb chops or | garlic (optional) |
| ½ lb. lamb | 1 cup rice (or a bit more, if they |
| 2 large onions | are hungry) |
| raisins (optional) | herbs, salt, pepper, bay leaf |

*Accompaniment:* 1 large can peeled tomatoes, half carton yoghourt

Cut the lean meat from the lamb into little pieces; put all the
bits you have removed – bone, fat, etc. – in a small pan with
4 cups water, and boil for 15 mins. with the lid on, meanwhile chopping onions. Put a dessertspoon of butter in a
saucepan. Brown the little pieces of lean meat and the
chopped onions. After 5 mins. or a little more, add the rice
and turn it in the fat until it is transparent. Now add the
liquid you have made from the lamb remains (keeping back
lumps and bits) – there should be at least 2 cups. Bubble
gently without a lid 20 mins. Next day heat up very gently
with a little more water and some more butter, but DON'T
LET IT BOIL. When it is hot, remove from ring, and quickly
heat up can of tomatoes, crushing them with a fork to make a
purée. Add yoghourt at the last minute (or cream, if you
don't like the sour taste of yoghourt) and hand round with
the lamb.

This can also be done the same day, except for the matter
of frying smelly onions. (45 mins.)

*The Dish* (So called because my flat-mate and I cooked
almost nothing else for nearly two years. It is absolutely
foolproof. We left it on all night once by mistake, and
it still made a lovely ragoût. For four on its own; six
with rice.)

| | |
|---|---|
| 1 lb. braising steak | 4 onions |
| 1 aubergine or 1 head celery | 1 pimento |
| flour, bay leaf, herbs, tomato | 2 leeks |
| paste (essential) | ¼ lb. mushrooms |

The point is that you can vary the vegetables, so long as you
keep in the onions and pimento, and make sure the rest are
interesting (i.e. not turnips).

Cut the beef into slices, and beat the flour (mixed with a
little salt and pepper) into it thoroughly. Chop up all the
vegetables. Heat 2 tablespoons olive oil in heavy pan, and
turn the slices of meat in it till all is brown. Add vegetables,
mixing all thoroughly together and putting the tomato paste

among the layers – about 1 dessertspoon in all. (A little wine or beer makes it, if possible, even nicer.) Add about 2 tablespoons water, and cook over lowest possible gas 2½ hrs.

If you can serve rice with it, these quantities will do six. (3 hrs.)

## *Gringo Beef* (Invented by mistake for something Mexican or Hawaiian. Only the most Americanized Pacific Islander would recognize it now. For four.)

| | |
|---|---|
| 1 lb. braising steak | 2 onions |
| 1 pimento | 4 rings pineapple (tinned or fresh) |
| 2 tomatoes | or chunks |
| tomato paste | pinch chilli powder |
| salt and herbs | 1 tablespoon flour |

Beat flour into beef as in preceding recipe, and brown in oil. Remove from pan; brown onions for 5 mins. Put back meat and add everything else. Simmer 1½ hrs or longer if possible. You can add more chilli powder if you like it, but watch out – one grain too much, and you go around with your mouth open for a week. (2 hrs or more.)

## *Carbonnade of Beef* (uses old beer; for four, with vegetable)

| | |
|---|---|
| ¾ lb.–1 lb. stewing or braising beef | 2 onions |
| herbs, salt, tomato paste | up to ½ pint beer |
| pepper | oil or butter |
| 1 tablespoon flour | bay leaf |

Cut meat into pieces and beat if tough-looking. Brown it in fat. Remove meat from pan, and brown the chopped-up onions. Sprinkle flour. Add beer and enough liquid to make total up to ½ pint. Simmer, with lid off, 5 mins. Add a tablespoon tomato paste, all other seasonings, and the meat. Simmer gently 2 hrs.

If fat forms on the surface when it is cold, remove it carefully before re-heating. This one needs a vegetable with it – or you could make potato dumplings (see page 50) and heat them up in it. (2½ hrs.)

## Beef Olives (for four)

4 thin slices of braising steak
4 potatoes
1 teaspoon chopped parsley
1 tablespoon oil or bacon fat

3 tablespoons breadcrumbs
mixed herbs; meat extract
  (optional)
1 tablespoon flour

Get the butcher to slice the meat thinly; beat out thin when you get it home, and cut into strips – two per person. Mix herbs, crumbs, parsley, salt, and pepper with a little milk; place a spoonful on each strip; roll up and peg with headless matchstick. Melt fat in pan; stir in flour, and add enough water to make a thick gravy. Add a little meat extract if you like. Lay in the beef olives, and the potatoes cut in small pieces. Simmer over very low gas $1\frac{1}{2}$–2 hrs. (2–$2\frac{1}{4}$ hrs.)

## Paupiettes de Bœuf (for four)

1 lb. beef – braising, or sliced
  from a roast
a piece lemon peel
parsley, salt, pepper, herbs

$\frac{1}{4}$ lb. mushrooms
2 onions
2 dessertspoons bread-
  crumbs
potatoes (optional)

Fry onion chopped fine for 5 mins. Add chopped washed mushrooms and fry 4 mins. more. Make a mixture with this and everything else except the beef. Proceed as for beef olives. Add a dollop of French mustard to water. Simmer 1 hr at least, with potatoes around if you like. ($1\frac{1}{2}$ hrs or more.)

## Goulash (with potato dumplings)

1 lb. braising steak (or veal or pork)
4 tomatoes, peeled
$\frac{1}{2}$–$\frac{3}{4}$ carton sour cream (essential)
4 onions *or* 3 leeks

*and*

1 pimento
  (optional)
paprika (essential)
salt, pepper, oil
1 teaspoon meat
  extract

4 large potatoes, 1 dessertspoon flour, 1 teaspoon butter

Cut fat and gristle off meat, beat it, and brown it in oil. Remove from pan and fry roughly chopped onions till transparent. Add half a cup water with meat extract dissolved in it; then the salt, pepper, and 1 dessertspoon paprika. Stir. Add herbs and a bay leaf and the meat. Simmer very gently 2 hrs, and cook the potatoes the night before the dinner, too. ($2\frac{1}{2}$ hrs.)

Next day, mash potatoes, mix with flour and butter, and form into little dumplings. As you heat the goulash slowly over a low gas, sit the dumplings on top for 15 mins. At last minute add sour cream (under the dumplings as far as possible); and be sure it does not boil at all after that. (20 mins.)

## *Blanquette de Veau* (for four)

| | |
|---|---|
| 1 lb. stewing veal | 2 onions |
| $\frac{1}{4}$ lb. mushrooms or mushroom stalks | 1 tablespoon |
| herbs, bay leaf, salt, pepper | butter |
| lemon juice | 1 tablespoon flour |
| | 1 egg yolk |

First trim all bits of fat and skin off veal. Cut in pieces and put it in pan with water; bring to boil, and throw out water. (This is to remove the revolting scum that will appear.) Now put the veal, the halved onions, the herbs, salt, pepper, and bay leaf in some more water, and boil gently until the veal is tender, which may be 20 mins. or 50. Boil *gently* – just bubbling, no more. Now melt butter in other pan (or, if the same, empty all contents into bowl first). Stir in flour. Gradually add the liquid the veal has been cooking in, keeping back pieces. When smooth and still reasonably thick, add the mushrooms (if stalks, very finely chopped), simmer 7 mins., add veal.

Next day, boil some potatoes. Then put the potatoes on a plate over the veal while it *very gently* warms up. At the last moment, stir in first the egg yolk, then a good squeeze of lemon.

Eat a green salad afterwards. ($1-1\frac{1}{2}$ hrs first day.)

## Osso Buco (for four)

1 shin of veal, sawn in pieces 2 in. thick
4 onions (optional)
4 or more tomatoes (essential)
twist of lemon peel

salt, pepper, herbs, garlic (optional)
1 glass white wine (essential or red permissible)
olive oil

Dust in flour and brown the four pieces of shin which have most meat on them in olive oil on all sides. Add onions, and let them colour. Add peeled tomatoes, herbs, wine. Simmer 1 hr or more. Serve with rice. ($1\frac{1}{2}$ hrs.)

## Pork and Aubergine Casserole (for four)

4 large pork chops
2 medium aubergines
2 heads celery (or 1 large tin)
1 small onion

1 teaspoon paprika
1 pinch cinnamon (optional)
herbs, salt, pepper

Brown pork chops in oil, after cutting off excess fat. Add sliced aubergine, and brown that. Add everything else, and cook gently for an hour. Next day, cook rice (by method 2 on page 78) and gently reheat casserole while rice stands by fire. ($1\frac{1}{4}$ hrs.)

## Prune Pork (for four)

1 lb. tenderloin of pork
2 cooking apples
8–10 soaked prunes

6–8 medium potatoes
meat extract
salt, pepper, herbs

Cut pork into four pieces, and make a slit in each. (You may be able to get the butcher to do it for you.) Peel and chop apples. Chop prunes. Add a herb or two to mixture of prunes and apples, and stuff each piece of pork; peg up opening with a couple of headless matchsticks. Brown very thoroughly in oil or butter or bacon fat. Put potatoes around, cut into pieces the size of small new potatoes. Pour over a

cup of water with a teaspoon of meat extract dissolved in it.
Simmer 1 hr. (Remove matchsticks before serving.) (1¼ hrs.)

## Cold Salmon (cooked the day before to make sure it is really cold – for four)

| | |
|---|---|
| 2 lb. good salmon, fresh, uncooked (salmon trout is OK) | 1 onion herbs, vinegar, salt, pepper, parsley |

If you are relying on your salmon as the main dish, it must
be quite perfect. This means cooking it in what is called a
*court bouillon*. Put all the herbs you can find, a tablespoonful
of vinegar, salt, pepper, and onion into about 2 pints of
water and boil them for 10 mins. minimum, longer if you
have time. Then, *and not till then*, lower the gas so that the
water is only just simmering – under boiling point– and put
in the salmon. Let it cook ¼ hr and cool in the liquid. You
can also make your mayonnaise the day before (see page 103).
With a fresh lettuce and cucumber, nothing could be nicer.
(30 mins.)

### OTHER SUGGESTIONS

There are some dishes which were simple enough to be included in Part One which are quite nice enough for you to
serve to your guests. Here is a list of possibilities, with
necessary adaptations:

MEDITERRANEAN FISH: See page 95. Double the quantities and leave out the onion because of the smell.

FRIED SOLE: See page 97. Allow two fillets per person
and serve with Tartare Sauce (see page 170) and a lemon.

POT ROAST: See page 84. If you are entertaining Category
3 people. Start it in plenty of time on the same day.

WIENER SCHNITZEL: See page 85. A lovely quick dish.
Allow one small escalope per person, and don't forget to
beat it. Do the dipping, and get the mess out of the way,
before your guests appear.

ITALIAN PORK CHOPS: See page 91. Recipe is for two; double it up if you are doing it for four. Could do the night before.

(*And any others you yourself like and feel confident about when cooking.*)

## TO BE MADE THE SAME DAY

### Stuffed Chicken (for two)

| | |
|---|---|
| 1 small chicken | ½ cup water and meat extract |
| ¼ lb. sausage meat | herbs, bay leaf, salt, pepper |
| 4 potatoes | |

Buy a chicken from which someone else has removed the guts. Fill it with sausage meat. Heat fat in pan – butter if you can possibly manage it – and brown the chicken thoroughly on all sides. Slice potatoes thin, and brown them slightly too. Now add the water, meat extract, herbs, etc. Put the lid on, and leave it on a low gas for at least ½ hr while you get on with other things. (45 mins.)

### Chicken and Peas (for two)

| | |
|---|---|
| 2 large or 4 small pieces of chicken (frozen is O.K.) | 1 small packet frozen peas |
| 4 sliced potatoes | mint, salt, pepper, butter |

Heat a tablespoon of butter in heavy pan. Turn chicken pieces till brown on all sides; add potato slices, and turn them till coated with butter. After 10 mins. add peas and mint. (It will sputter; never mind.) Cook with lid on for 15 mins., or until chicken is tender. (35 mins.)

### Chicken à la King (for four)

| | |
|---|---|
| 1 medium-sized cooked chicken | 1 chicken soup cube |
| ½ lb. mushrooms (*or* ¼ lb. mushrooms and ¼ lb. chopped stalks) | 1 tablespoon butter |
| | 1 tablespoon flour |
| 1 small tin pimentoes | 1 egg yolk |

Fry chopped mushrooms in the butter for six minutes. Remove mushrooms and shake flour into fat. Stir. Gradually add 1 cup water in which chicken cube has dissolved. (A little cream or top of the milk is good too.) Cook 5 mins. Add mushrooms, chicken cut in boneless pieces, the chopped cooked pimentoes, and salt and pepper. Cook another 5 mins. Lift off gas, and stir in egg yolk.

This will sit quite happily while you heat up pre-cooked rice, or pre-cooked potatoes in butter. (20 mins.)

## *Bœuf Stroganoff* (for four)

1 lb. good steak
4 tomatoes
¼ lb. mushrooms
1 teaspoon French mustard
4–6 cooked sliced potatoes
herbs, bay leaf, salt, pepper
1 small carton sour cream

Cut the beef into very thin small slices, and beat them out with a bottle or saucer edge or your wooden spoon. Dust them in flour. Melt butter in pan. Add washed and sliced mushrooms, peeled tomatoes in chunks, herbs, and potatoes. Simmer gently for 6 mins. Push to side of pan, raise heat slightly, and fry beef strips 2 mins. each side. Lower gas, add mustard, salt, pepper, and 4 dessertspoons sour cream. Stir once thoroughly and remove from gas. (25 mins.)

## *Saltimbocca* (for four)

2 very large or 4 medium escalopes of veal
¼ lb. mushroom stalks
2 slices of ham
4 tomatoes (optional)
2 tablespoons grated Parmesan cheese
meat extract and water (optional)

Chop mushroom stalks fine and fry gently for 5 mins. Meanwhile beat out escalopes flat and halve slices of ham. Fry the tomatoes while you make sandwiches with a slice of veal, a half slice of ham, a spoonful of mushroom, a dollop of grated cheese, and another slice of veal for each. Fry the sandwiches for 3 mins. on each side. (20 mins.)

## *Bolognese Cutlets with Fried Potatoes* (for four)

| | |
|---|---|
| 6 medium-sized potatoes | breadcrumbs |
| 2 large or 4 small escalopes | 2 large slices ham (optional |
| 1 egg | grated Parmesan cheese |

First peel and slice potatoes, and start them frying in the pan. Meanwhile beat out the escalopes as thin as they will go. Beat up egg on plate, put breadcrumbs on another plate, and dip escalopes first in egg then in breadcrumbs. Now get rid of the mess, and drain the nearly-cooked potatoes on clean newspaper. You can stop at this stage and leave the rest till the last minute if you like. Melt some more butter if necessary. Fry crumbed escalopes 2 mins. each side, medium heat. Lower gas, add potatoes. Put a half slice of ham and a spoonful of grated cheese on each escalope, and scoop up butter over each. Put on lid (or lay a plate over the top) and leave for 4 mins. on low gas, to melt the cheese. First stage 15 mins. Second stage 10 mins. (25 mins.)

## *Veal Cutlets and Cream* (for four)

| | |
|---|---|
| 4 veal cutlets | 1 carton single cream |
| 1 large packet frozen beans | butter |
| 6 pre-cooked potatoes | |

First cook the frozen beans, and drain. Now fry the veal cutlets in butter, turning from time to time, for 15 mins. on medium flame. Put in beans and potatoes. Cook 3 or 4 mins. to heat up. Push all food to side of pan. Tilt pan, add cream to butter, and stir. Mix with food over low heat. Serve. (30 mins.)

## *Lamb Orloff* (for four)

| | |
|---|---|
| 6 lamb chops | 1 tablespoon butter (or more) |
| ½ lb. mushrooms | 1 tablespoon flour |
| 1 tablespoon grated cheese | 1 cup milk |

Cut good parts from chops. Fry gently, 10 mins. After 5 mins. put in washed chopped mushrooms. Remove mushrooms and chops, and shake flour into the fat; stir; gradually add milk, and stir till thick. Add cheese. Simmer 5 mins. Put back lamb and mushrooms and simmer another 5 mins. (30 mins.)

## FISH AND SEAFOOD

Fish can be rather dull for company. If it says wine, either play fair and put in the wine, or choose something else.

### *Shrimp Wiggle* (for four)

| | |
|---|---|
| 1 large and 1 small packet shrimps | ¼ lb. chopped green olives |
| 1 large packet frozen peas | |
| 1 dessertspoon butter | 1 egg yolk |
| 1 dessertspoon flour | 1 cup rice |
| 1 cup milk | salt, pepper |

First cook rice (see page 78). While it stands, make a white sauce (see page 42), melting the butter, adding the flour, and gradually stirring in the milk. Add peas, shrimps, olives. Simmer very gently 20 mins. Put another half cupful of water in the rice and set it to reheat, boiling, for 3 or 4 mins. while you remove wiggle from flame and stir in egg yolk. (45 mins.)

### *Fish in White Wine* (for four)

| | |
|---|---|
| 4 *large* fillets cod, plaice, sole, or even mackerel | 1 tablespoon flour |
| ½ cup milk | 4 tomatoes (optional, but they look good) |
| ½ cup white wine | herbs, salt, pepper |
| 1 tablespoon butter | |

Unfreeze fish if necessary, and remove any bones and black skin if possible. Make white sauce with butter, flour, milk, and wine (see page 42); cut down the milk slightly if it seems

to be getting sloshy. Add salt, pepper, herbs. Stir. Add fish.
Lay the tomatoes, sliced, on top. Bubble very gently 10–15
mins. (30 mins.)


## Crab Casserole (a sure-fire winner for four)

| | |
|---|---|
| 2 medium size tins of crab | 1 tablespoon butter |
| ¼ lb. mushrooms | ½ cup milk |
| ¼ lb. mushroom stalks | salt, pepper, ½ teaspoon |
| 1 wineglass white wine | mustard |
| 1 tablespoon flour | tarragon (optional) |

Wash and clean mushrooms, cutting stalks fine. Remove
white membrane pieces from tinned crab. Make a white
sauce (see page 42) with the butter, flour, wine, and milk.
Add salt and pepper, mushrooms, crab, and simmer gently
for ½ hr. Serve *with* but not *on* toast. (45 mins.)


## Scallops and Mushrooms (for four)

| | |
|---|---|
| 6 scallops | 8 small potatoes |
| ¼ lb. mushrooms | 2 spring onions *or* ½ small onion |
| ¼ lb. mushroom stalks | parsley; salt, pepper |

First peel potatoes and put on to boil for 15 mins. Meanwhile
wash mushrooms, chopping stalks very fine. Remove any
oddments from scallops – you eat the red and the white meat
– and slice in two. When potatoes are nearly cooked, remove
and drain. Fry onion gently till golden, add mushrooms, and
fry very gently another 5 mins. Shake 1 tablespoon flour
over and stir hard. Add ½ cup milk. Stir till thick. Add
scallops and potatoes and simmer 15–20 mins. (35–40 mins.)


## Sybil's Scallops (for four)

| | |
|---|---|
| 6 scallops, white and red meat | 1 tablespoon flour |
| ¼ lb. mushrooms (or more, if | 1 cup creamy milk or |
| no potatoes or rice served) | more |
| 1 tablespoon butter | parsley |

Put the cleaned scallops with the mushrooms (big ones chopped, little ones left whole) with the butter and cook *very gently* for 10 mins. Then lift them out on to a plate, and add the flour to the butter remaining in the pan. Stir in the milk till it thickens, add the parsley, and simmer 5 mins. Put back scallops and mushrooms, and simmer another 5 mins. (30 mins.)

## Lobster Newburg (for two)

| | |
|---|---|
| 1 large tin lobster (*or* the cooked meat of one fresh lobster) | 2 egg yolks |
| | 1 glass sherry |
| 1 bottle single cream | salt, pepper |

Beat the egg yolks thoroughly in a cup. Put on a pan of boiling water, and sit your bowl on the top of it, with the cream in the bowl. After a minute or two add the beaten egg yolks, stirring hard. Stir for 3–4 mins., then add sherry, salt, pepper, and finally the lobster. IT MUST NOT BOIL. Serve and eat just as it is, with a green salad to follow. (15 mins.)

## Sauce Tartare (if you should decide to serve fried fish)

> '*I know what they put in the sauce tartare*
> *The sauce tartare in the restaurant car*'

sang an old man in a musical, who could not consequently be sacked. Well, so do I; but this is different.

First make some mayonnaise (see page 103). It really is worth the effort. Then add a teaspoonful of chopped capers, a half teaspoon of French mustard, extra salt and pepper, and even a little more vinegar if necessary; and chopped chives if you can manage it. This sauce will lift ordinary fish to the entertaining level.

✳✳✳✳✳✳✳✳✳✳✳✳✳✳✳✳✳✳✳✳✳✳✳✳✳

## CHAPTER 14

# *The Last Course*

IN the play *The Shrike*, the hero is entertaining his girl to dinner and she says, 'What's for dessert?' And there is no dessert and he tries to commit suicide. This is an extreme view. If you have given your guests a starting course and a main course, that will often do fine, especially if you can break out and hand round some attractive chocolates or crystallized fruit with the coffee. When friends ask 'Can I bring anything?' and you hesitate to suggest wine, sweets are one thing that you can unblushingly ask for.

Alternatively, you can hand round one of the sweet objects (on page 128–9) which are half-way between sweets and a sweet, a *bonne bouche* and a pudding, candy and dessert.

But if you are leaving out the last course, you must have coffee. You could, however, compromise between coffee and an ice by giving them iced coffee (see page 131). Nothing is nicer in summer.

If you are making a proper pudding, there's only one thing to beware of: if you have a mousse or a summer pudding sitting in your bowl, you cannot then use it for salad. So plan the meal for one or the other. Remember cream makes any pudding a bit nicer, and small biscuits can be handed with a fluffy pudding if you suspect that they have had only just enough to eat on the other two courses.

One way in which you can turn your gas ring to advantage is to cook *at* your guests, if you are feeling very confident. Make a rum omelette or a zabaione. But *only* if you have done it often enough before to be sure it won't go up in flames.

If you produce cheese for your final course, remember that people are apt to have strong views about cheese and it is as well to provide a choice. Have one *firm* cheese (Cheddar, Cheshire, Caerphilly, Double Gloucester, Wensleydale, Dutch, Edam, Gruyère, Bel Paese, Port Salut – it's a matter of texture, this, not nationality); one '*blue*' (Roquefort, Gorgonzola, Stilton, Danish Blue); and either one *sloppy* one (Camembert, Valmeuse, Brie) or a *creamy* cheese (Petit Suisse, Demi Sel, St Ivel, ordinary cream cheese). One way round all this is to have a Bresse Blue, which is both blue and a cream cheese; though even then it is as well to have a firm cheese as well.

Petit Suisses are a good risk, because some people love to eat them with cinnamon and sugar – but this is more a female fancy than a male.

And whatever you serve, do let me repeat: fresh, crusty bread, or good biscuits; cheese fresh and good of its kind; fresh butter and plenty of it.

CHAPTER 15

# Drink and Parties

(This chapter is contributed by a man)

IT should be news to no one that red wine goes with red meat and most game; white wine with fish, veal, and the sweet courses. More to the point, perhaps, is that white wine goes with carpets; red wine only with floors you can wipe clean or don't need to care about.

Assuming that anybody who drinks alone has been at it long enough to know what they like and how, the question of what to serve is entirely a matter for guest evenings and parties. Basically, play to the carpet rule unless you're quite sure you're entertaining non-spillers.

There is a vast amount of prestige attached to wine drinking; and since you can't ignore all of it, you may as well get the benefit of it where you can afford it. But remember that most people – even those who make a living writing about wine – know less about it than they care to let on. There are just too many vineyards, châteaux, importers, bottlers, labellers, 'vintage years', 'bad years', and in short too many different wines from different places, for anybody to know all of them and steer clear of Alcoholics Anonymous.

By now wines are coming in from all over the world and you can buy not only to suit your pocket but your politics. With most cheap wines the year doesn't matter much: they're meant to be drunk young. The best approach is to shop around until you've found something in the right price bracket, then buy half a bottle, drink it, and if it seems all right, go back and buy what you need. But go back to the *same* place: different shipments may taste quite different.

In general, you'll probably find even the cheapest French

wines less good value than Spanish or Chilean, and German-style wines come cheaper from Yugoslavia.

With Italian wines, mostly red and white chiantis, you're paying for the nice bottle in the fancy straw doodat. If you like to buy one bottle and thereafter decant your other wines into it, I leave that to your conscience – which shouldn't be too much trouble, if it's another chianti bought in Soho in ordinary bottles at ordinary prices. But don't forget north Italian wines like Valpolicella and Bardolino as an alternative.

Red wine improves a great deal by having the cork taken out of it an hour or two before you want to drink it, to give it time to 'breathe' at room temperature. (Trying to heat it up in front of the gas-fire is no substitute for this.) White wine and rosé should be cooled – wrap a piece of wet paper round the bottle and the evaporation will cool your wine.

In gauging how much you need, one full bottle will do a good glass and a half for four people. That should see you through a quiet dinner: but it may be skimpy if you are handing out nothing first. If you are going to get more, get a full bottle: halves look mean. If you are trying to make do with one, top up their glasses before they've finished the first dose. A low trick, but makes it look more.

Drinking before a meal means either spirits (see under 'Spirits', below) or getting in a bottle of sherry. This costs more than wine, but you dole it out in smaller quantities and one glass is enough if you're prompt with the meal. One bottle can last several guest nights – if you can keep away from it in the meantime.

South African is OK in most circles by now, otherwise Spanish. The safest species to get is 'medium' – a light amber colour. The best prestige value is 'dry' – a golden yellow.

If you're serving brandy after the meal, get a quarter bottle, pour it into the smallest glasses you can find, and brew the coffee up fast. There's absolutely no need to give the whole works, though; and it may be better to skip the brandy in favour of a second bottle of wine. Cheaper, too.

And it's certainly better to skip the brandy to make sure the sherry and wine are drinkable.

By and large, it is a bad rule to buy the cheapest of anything, and a good rule, when faced with the temptation, to buy the best of something cheaper. Thus, give an expensive South African sherry rather than the cheapest possible Spanish, and vintage cider rather than bargain-counter champagne. The happy fact is that nobody will know you thought of giving them champagne, anyway.

## PARTIES

There are only two firm rules for parties: the carpet rule redoubled in spades; and *don't mix the booze*. It may seem fun to serve a big bowl of hell-brew full of odds and ends of orange, apple, and cucumber, but it dooms the party from the start. The guests don't know what they're drinking, and therefore don't know how to drink it. They either sip it delicately and end up three hours later stone cold sober, unconversational, and feeling swindled, or they gulp it down and are sick on the carpet.

If you simply offer them straight drinks – beer, wine, spirits, or a choice of all three – they know where they are, and needn't stay soberer or get tighter than they want to. You can't very well stop a man getting drunk if he's that way inclined, but you *can* stop him getting drunk by accident.

## BEER

Beer comes in four ways: from the bottle, from the can, from the barrel, and from the tap. In the bottle you can get light (a sort of super-bitter) or brown (a super-mild). Don't bother with half-pint bottles: they're too much trouble to carry and too many to sit around looking dead the next morning. Most people prefer light to brown; and allow three pints per person for an average-length party. But don't go much above four in any circumstances. It will all be drunk, but only because guests look on undrunk beer as a challenge.

Don't gaily whip the stopper out of a bottle the moment you've carried it upstairs: and don't let bottled beer stand stoppered near the fire. In either case it will squirt to the ceiling.

But despite what the brewers say, most bottled beer can be bounced around in a shopping bag or on the back seat of a car, and providing the bottles are full to start with, and are allowed to stand in the cool for half an hour before opening, it'll suffer hardly at all.

Canned beer seems to me inordinately expensive. However, in the last few years most brewers have started putting out ordinary draught beer in large tins, now mostly in four-pint sizes. This is easy and cheap, the only snag being that the undrunk goes off quickly and each brewer usually only does one size of tin. So calculate carefully how much you need and then shop around.

All beer tastes better the colder it gets, so if you can shove it in the landlady's fridge for half an hour first, that will improve matters. But probably you'll be doing your best not to let her know you've got beer and friends in; so cool as for white wine, with wet newspaper.

You can buy ordinary draught beer by the barrel: a 'pin' holds 36 pints. A 'firkin' holds, and costs, just twice as much. This is slightly cheaper than you can buy beer across a pub bar, and the men (from either the brewer's or the wine stores – you can order it at either) will lug it upstairs, install it, and tap it for you. If you're doing this, make sure it can stand for at least twenty-four hours before drinking starts. You'll never drink anything fouler than shook-up barrelled beer – and never eat anything fouler, either: it'll be full of hops and other vegetation. Most people, again, prefer bitter to mild in draught beer, although this varies with what part of the country you live in.

Two things argue against a barrel: some fool always leaves the tap running; and even if you don't spill a drop, somehow the place smells like a brewery for days. If you're getting a barrel anyway, allow at least four pints per person, remembering that draught beer is weaker than bottled.

And finally, you can always go down to the local with an armful of bottles and have them filled from the tap. It costs what it does across the counter and while the duchess doesn't do it, plenty of others do. And despite the pundits, it doesn't suffer much in transit, for the simple reason that most pubs don't keep their beer well enough for a little more suffering to make any difference.

(Actually, beer now comes in a fifth way: home brewed. This can be very good, but probably not the first time you make it. So don't trust your own, or anybody else's effort unless it's backed by real experience.)

## WINE

Wine is a perfectly sound drink to serve at any party. Remember the carpet, but don't bother too much about the label as long as it tastes all right. One bottle to one person is over-generous for any party.

## SPIRITS

Spirits cost money. Pubs reckon getting 32 measures from one bottle (so you can work out a rough idea of their gross profit), but I shouldn't go giving your friends pub-sized measures if you want them to stay friends.

Gin is the safest: more women like it than like whisky, and men will drink anything, anyway. Anybody who drinks gin drinks tonic, so add at least six bottles of tonic water (the 'split' size are the best economically) and don't bother with any other 'mixers'. And *don't* try to mix dry martinis: there are as many ways to mix this as there are people drinking it, and the only thing you can be sure of is that you'll get it wrong.

Vodka is something of a 'fashionable' drink and, like most fashions, you'll find some people won't touch it. Offer with tonic, as for gin.

With whisky get a syphon of soda water and have a jug of cool clean water (stick a saucer over it) for those who prefer water with it.

Personal capacities vary, but most men can get through a quarter bottle without too much of a struggle. For a mixed party, allow five or six people to a full bottle of spirits; and if there's any left over, it'll keep. Shops will always let you have spirits on the 'sale or return' principle – this stops you worrying yourself into fits about running out, but may result in the last four determined drinkers having a bottle each. Buy a half bottle if the occasion demands no more; but quarters, and certainly 'miniatures', are poor economics.

Buying gin you can hardly go wrong; vodka is trickier since prices vary widely, sometimes for no good reason and sometimes because the strength varies: make sure you get something in the 65–70 proof range. Whisky is more difficult still since different brands taste quite different. Beware of brands with too-Scottish names, and particularly those that seem to be stocked only in half bottles. Otherwise, buy the cheapest you can find for party use, but be ready to pay more and get a good name – Teacher's, Bell's, Dewars – for more reflective after-dinner sipping.

There is nothing against having beer for the men and gin for the women – if you can keep the men away from the gin.

A quart of cider is one of the cheapest ways of taking alcohol aboard. Most women prefer it to beer; and men will drink it if there's nothing else.

For non-drinkers, lay in a few pineapple and tomato juices – tins are cheaper than bottles – and reckon that anyone can get through a large tin in an evening.

Most wine stores, if you're buying the booze from them, will lend you all the glasses you want free and charge you only for the ones you break: the economics of that depends on your friends.

And again – don't mix the booze.

Please.

## WHERE TO BUY?

Thanks to the abolition of resale price maintenance, booze is a great area for bargain hunting. Rule one is never buy from a pub, and so are most of the other rules; pubs don't want to encourage drinking at home and charge accordingly.

The cheapest places are the cut-price wine-and-spirit stores, particularly for spirits and sherries. The snag with the wines may be that they are odd-job lots and the proprietor may know nothing about them – or be able to re-order them.

Ordinary wine stores are forced to keep their prices reasonably competitive, and are good places to talk to the shopkeeper about wines. He wants you as a regular customer so his advice will probably be good.

Ordinary grocers and supermarkets may now stock a whole range of drinks, but keep a sharp eye on the prices and don't trust their advice: the man giving it may have been selling baked beans last week.

The big supermarket chains do a number of 'own-brand' cheap red and white wines, which are often good value – particularly in the litre-size bottles. The actual taste may vary from year to year since the wine itself may come from a different country.

✳✳✳✳✳✳✳✳✳✳✳✳✳✳✳✳✳✳✳✳✳✳✳✳

# Epilogue

THERE is perhaps only one man in Britain who has wholly
solved the problem of eating well in a bedsitter. When I
went to visit him, a compound smell of celery, garlic, and
freshly ground coffee – the essential smell of a French
kitchen – met me faintly as I climbed the stairs. There was a
sound of steak-bashing from within, and when I knocked on
the outside of his door, a bag of vegetables fell heavily to the
ground on the inside.

The whole room spoke food. As Marcus set about making
coffee, and settled me comfortably on what later turned out
to be a haybox, I had time to take in the details. There was a
row of growing herbs on the windowsill, a row of cookery
books on the mantelpiece; and along the top of the books
there lay, like a withered snake, a single vanilla pod. At one
end of this mantelpiece, which was broad, a large jar of bee
wine was in full activity, the bees with awful deliberation
floating very slowly up and down. At the other, Marcus had
set a Camembert to mature. On every wall there were hooks,
from which hung knives and saucepans, and a string of
onions, and another of garlic, a salad-shaker and a grater,
and two kinds of egg whisk, and a bunch of bay leaves. The
only picture was a Victorian still life in oils, showing a brace
of freshly killed pheasant with some vegetables. There was a
beer barrel in one corner, with an old slipper under the tap
to catch the drips; and in another some curd cheese was
draining into a small shaving bowl through a sock. The open
wardrobe door revealed, beneath the somewhat agricultural
jackets and trousers, a box of earth in which some mushrooms were growing.

As Marcus strode round the room, gripping the coffee-grinder to his chest, and pausing occasionally to prod the sock or stir the simmering pot on the gas ring, he told me something of his story. He had been a chemist, working regular hours in a perfectly serious laboratory; and then, in response to a need of his own, he had invented and patented a chemically operated refrigerator which needed no gas or electricity; a model of this now stood in the shadows near his wardrobe. The invention had sold, though not spectacularly; Marcus was now eating entirely on the profits, and had given up regular work altogether in favour of food.

When I asked him '*How* do you manage to live so well in your bed-sitting-room?' he winced like a huntsman hearing a fox's brush called a tail.

'You mustn't *think* of it as a bed-sitting-room,' he said. '*I'm sleeping in the kitchen.*'

# Index

183